MEETINGS ARE WHERE
CAREERS ARE MADE
BY THOSE WHO
KNOW THE HIDDEN
AGENDAS, PINPOINT
THE POWER SPOTS,
ISOLATE THE
ADVERSARIES, AND
COME OUT ON TOP

SIMON
AND
SCHUSTER

THE
STRATEGY
OF
MEETINGS

GEORGE DAVID KIEFFER

New York
London
Toronto
Sydney
Tokyo

SIMON AND SCHUSTER and colophon are registered trademarks
of Simon & Schuster Inc.

Designed by Irving Perkins Associates
Manufactured in the United States of America

1   2   3   4   5   6   7   8   9   10

Library of Congress Cataloging-in-Publication Data
Kieffer, George David.
The strategy of meetings.

Includes index.
1. Meetings—Handbooks, manuals, etc.
2. Communication in management—Handbooks, manuals,
etc. 3. Leadership—Handbooks, manuals, etc.
I. Title.
AS6.K47   1988   658.4'563   88-4509
ISBN 0-671-61197-6

TO
JUDITH

CONTENTS

CONTENTS

INTRODUCTION
The Strategic Importance of Meetings

YOU'RE heading into a meeting. It may be down the hall, down the block, or across the nation. Maybe it's right in your own office. It could be to close a deal or to orient your staff. It could be to report to your boss or to discuss problems with fellow members of the PTA. Whatever the task, it must be important, for you've set aside everything else you might be doing in order to join with your meeting partners. And they've stopped everything else they were doing in order to meet with you.

The meeting you are about to attend will be the focus of enormous energies and pressures, some of which will be quickly seen, others of which will remain hidden. It will be the culmination of work that may have gone on for days or weeks, even years. It will be a catalyst for good ideas and bad ideas, for tasks and problems and opportunities and meetings to come.

Your meeting could be a quick victory or a long-term success. It could be an immediate bust or a failure recognized only with the passage of time. Your meeting partners may be working for you or against you. In any event, at stake are egos, profits, promotions, projects, perhaps the fate of whole companies.

You're heading into a meeting, and in that meeting you will either motivate or discourage, inform or confuse, persuade or fail to persuade. In the end, you will win or you will lose—for yourself, for your cause, and for your company or organization. You will actually accomplish something, or you will waste your time, your reputation, and a piece of your life. For no matter how much we may complain about them, meetings are absolutely *central* to business and professional life and thereby central to your career—to your own success or failure.

Meetings are the fulcrum for all commercial and noncommercial transactions, the central nervous system of an information society, the center stage for personal performance. Once you have made this connection, your attitude toward meetings must change forever. And once you perceive that meetings are perhaps the single most important "window" on business and professional life, the window through which we see and evaluate and are seen and evaluated, you will be far less casual about invitations to meet and far more demanding of the meetings you choose to call or attend.

The failure to make this fundamental connection has led many intelligent people to accept passively an endless round of unsuccessful and ineffective meetings in the mistaken belief that if they don't do any good, at least they don't do much harm. Nothing could be more false. Yet, as a lawyer and a businessman, and as an active participant on a great number of boards and commissions, I have encountered this ironic situation again and again: bright people attending foolish meetings; otherwise careful professionals managing careless and damaging meetings. Then one day I was asked to do a memorandum on how to manage meetings more successfully for new members coming on to a large public board. That memorandum led to a magazine interview on business and professional meetings; and finally, my attendance at one too many counterproductive meetings led to writing this book.

To get a broader perspective, I decided to talk with some of America's most successful and respected leaders in business, labor, industry, education, and government—many of whom are viewed as masters in the art of conducting meetings—to gain their insights into the subject. In speaking with over fifty of those leaders, two central points emerged. Number one, the skill to manage a meeting—to develop ideas, to motivate people, and to move people and ideas to positive action—is perhaps the most critical asset in any career. And number two, most professionals have had no real training in devising and managing an effective meeting; in fact, most professionals do not recognize the enormous impact their meetings have on their organizations and their careers.

For the purposes of this book, I have defined a "meeting" broadly as a business or professionally oriented gathering of two or more people. Of course, there are literally as many kinds of meetings as there are people who attend them. But, at root, the same basic rules of good management can be applied to all meetings. Sales meetings, staff meetings, negotiations, board meetings, large meetings, small meetings— whatever the size and style of the meeting, the fundamental principles are still the same. And they are applicable whether you are leading or attending a meeting.

This book is not intended to tell you everything you ever wanted to know about meetings. Rather, it is intended to encourage you to begin to think strategically about the meetings you lead or attend. In the process, you will learn how to avoid foolish meetings and how to restructure those you do attend to achieve your goals. You will learn to become more accomplished in the art of managing people and ideas in meetings to get what you want. And you will learn how to be a winner when it comes to your own business and professional meetings and therefore your career. Meetings are more fundamental to good management than most people think. If you're wasting this precious resource, you're hurting your career.

Part One

THE HIGH STAKES IN EVERY MEETING

There is more to this than meets the eye.

—ANONYMOUS

CHAPTER ONE

You Are Judged on How You Handle a Meeting

How many times have you gone to a meeting only to be frustrated, bored, or unimpressed? The same judgments are being made about you and your meetings by those with higher expectations.

Judgments about you and your overall abilities are made by others in every meeting you attend on the basis of how you manage that meeting, whether as a leader or participant. These judgments reflect conscious evaluations of your power, ability, skills, and potential for advancement within a company, organization, or profession. And as you move higher on any career ladder, you will encounter more and more people who have higher and higher requirements and expectations about your meeting skills.

In fact, increased responsibility in any organization

is actually granted to a large extent in consideration of one's ability to handle people and problems in meetings and you will not be promoted to the next level of authority and responsibility until you are perceived to have the skills necessary to handle meetings on that level. Likewise, a judgment is made about you by your peers and subordinates, who consciously and unconsciously alter their subsequent work with you based upon how you handle a meeting. That judgment, too, becomes more demanding as you move up the career and professional ladder.

Harold M. Williams is the former chief executive officer of Norton Simon Industries. He is also the former dean of the University of California at Los Angeles School of Management and served as chairman of the Securities Exchange Commission in the Carter administration. Williams is now President of the Getty Trust, governing the largest privately endowed museum in the world. He has worked in the worlds of business, education, government, and private foundations. No matter the field, he says, the same kinds of judgments are made. "Any time you're in a meeting," he states, "you're sending a message about who you are, what your abilities are, and what league you belong in." Williams looks carefully for that message, for it tells him who can accomplish something, who is worth listening to, and who can handle further responsibility. "Whether I'm dealing with employees or international business associates, I am always evaluating the people at the table with a view to future responsibilities and relationships."

Not long ago I met with an Indiana-based client

company (about $100 million in sales) and high-ranking officials of a state and a federal agency who were making a preliminary investigation of the company. The company had assembled about half a dozen of its middle- and upper-level management to answer questions from the government officials. I was charged with orchestrating the presentations and therefore had the opportunity to be briefed by the chairman and CEO about the qualities of each of our presenters. One presenter, who had a second-level position in a branch office, was described to me by the chairman as "very competent," but, he added "I'm not sure what kind of a job he can do with the government heavyweights." As it turned out, the employee impressed the so-called heavyweights tremendously, and when I happened to visit him three months later, he had been promoted to head that office. The CEO told me later, "He just showed me what he could do in a very sophisticated meeting. That was all it took. He was really good. But I honestly never thought of him as a lead guy before that meeting."

The judgments that are made are not limited to only the most serious and obvious meetings. Recently, the president of a large realty company in Los Angeles told me he was so impressed by the way a young father handled a meeting of parents of a children's Little League team that he offered him a good job in the company! "Look," he said, "I've had people working for me for years who still can't run a meeting. I can teach real estate value. I'm not sure I can teach how to deal with people."

WHY JUDGMENTS MUST BE MADE

It may seem unfair, even unwise, that anyone would decide whether or not you might be qualified for a choice assignment on the basis of a casual business lunch or a series of meetings of the local PTA; or that your employees' and associates' performance and subsequent treatment of you is altered by your conduct in a meeting. Of course, when working relationships continue over time, the importance of any one meeting diminishes. Yet general judgments about you will inevitably be made because how you handle a meeting reveals how you might handle a future job necessarily full of meetings. There are few visible bases on which to make judgments regarding managerial and leadership skills, and the ability to manage meetings is as accurate a reflection of such skills as one can find.

Meetings have always been an important part of work life, but they have become increasingly important over the last decade. The average professional or manager is now spending over 25 percent of his time in meetings. Upper- and middle-level managers spend over 40 percent of their time in meetings. Some senior executives spend four full days per week in meetings. With so much time devoted to meetings, judgments about meeting skills must be made. As former ITT Chairman Harold Geneen said, "It was in our meetings that we ran ITT." The implication: If you can't handle a meeting, you can't handle the company.

For good or bad, recent studies show a general move

toward more and longer meetings throughout business and professional life. The causes appear to be tied to the general trend to an information/service-based economy from an industrial economy, the growth in shared management and participatory democracy in the work place, increasing reliance on task-force management, and what social forecaster and author John Naisbitt has referred to as the need for more "high touch" in an increasingly high-tech environment. The authors of one recent study predict a further 5–9 percent increase in the frequency of meetings over the next five years. There is simply a greater demand for meetings.

This is certainly not to say that all meetings are necessary or beneficial. They are not. In fact, when so much time must be allocated to meetings, business and professional leaders must look for people with *total* meeting skills, including the skills to limit and shape the increasing demand for meetings. The person who meets at the wrong moment, or too often, or for too long is a liability. Therefore, for top people, any meeting becomes a window on the professional life and abilities of each participant, where one's imagination, responsiveness, judgment, and total skills are all on the table to be evaluated. "One can learn such things only by face-to-face interaction, not by reading reports," Geneen says. "Sitting in a meeting and talking with people, seeing them think aloud, answering questions, solving problems, you get an idea of their capabilities."

Former U.S. Senator and now successful businessman John Tunney goes further. "I believe anyone in management has something of an obligation to form these judgments about other people in meetings. Life is short and decisions about people must be made."

Summarizing a long discussion we had at his home, former U.S. Air Force Secretary Verne Orr was equally adamant. "Look," he said, "my job was largely managing people. So when I sought leadership, I looked for credentials, sure, but I really looked for people who could manage other people in meetings. It separates the wheat from the chaff."

A few minutes in a meeting can tell the meeting master far more than they might tell the average person. Obviously, he looks for strength of personality and leadership ability. But the master will also attempt to judge whether you are on top of the job or project, whether you can understand and manage people, events, and ideas or whether they manage you. Do you meet as a substitute for work or as a tool to get something done? Are you a passive participant wasting time or a focused manager? Can you prioritize? Do you listen? Can you handle more responsibility?

Sometimes the judgment is more sophisticated still. A university president I once knew seldom seemed to permit his vice presidents to finish answering questions from board members at meetings. One day a fellow board member, the venerable Ed Carter, founder of Carter Hawley Hale, Inc., turned to me and said, "You see, this guy just can't delegate. He's gotten himself into all sorts of trouble, and I must say I suspected it from the first time I saw him run a meeting."

IT USUALLY GETS DOWN TO A MEETING

You may work for weeks to prepare a report for a meeting of division heads and your boss. The only thing they may ever know about you and your report is how you manage that meeting. You may work for a year on a business deal that will succeed or fail on the basis of a single meeting. And you may have failed to win an appointment to a position you never knew was available because of your performance in a meeting you cannot even remember.

It is said that Jimmy Carter picked Walter Mondale to run (and eventually serve) as his vice president primarily on the basis of a meeting between the two of them in Plains, Georgia. Richard Nixon's political career was aided immeasurably by two meetings—the congressional hearings in the famous Alger Hiss perjury case and the "kitchen debate" with Soviet leader Nikita Khrushchev. His ability to understand the real audience—the American public—ultimately won him the vice presidency. The impression created by President John Kennedy in his meeting with Khrushchev is cited by historians as having encouraged the Soviet leader to put missiles in Cuba, nearly precipitating World War III.

These relatively brief moments and hundreds of thousands like them that involve ordinary people day in and day out become the basis upon which profound judgments are made. For you are telling peers, subordinates, and superiors whether you are good enough to be trusted with their companies, their goals, and their careers.

SENDING SIGNALS

In every meeting we attend, we send signals. We tend to believe that people around us know far more about us and our abilities than they actually do. But what they really do is interpret those signals: signs of self-respect, organization, confidence, competence, success, and the ability to execute. The more perceptive the individual, the more sophisticated are the signs he both perceives and sends.

"It is almost like giving me a hidden television camera in their office," according to Don Gevirtz, chairman of the board and chief executive officer of the Foothill Group, a financial services company. "My employees start to forget I'm there—and that's good. I try to watch for signs that they can manage other people and information, that they can think. How did they prepare? Do they understand what I'm trying to accomplish when I'm leading a meeting, and can they help me get there? I can tell a great deal about leadership capacity simply watching an employee attend a meeting."

The simple job interview suggests how important a single meeting can be, compared to other criteria, when you're looking for a job. For example, each year the most prestigious law firms in the country look for students at the best law schools for associate positions. I have been involved in this process on behalf of

24

my law firm for nearly fifteen years now. The competition among students and among law firms is very keen. Yet I'm always surprised by how little we or the other law firms really know about the students we hire. We go on a partial law school transcript and an interview. Signals. That's it! Good grades are the minimum. What we see in the interview is what we *think* we'll get. We don't know how hard the student works, how creative he may be, how persuasive she is, and how good with clients they might be—except as each student presents himself or herself in the interview. All we can do is look for signs that reflect diligence, creativity, or good fellowship. On the basis of that look, we make a decision. Now compare that to the time and energy you put into buying a car. You watch TV, check the ads, visit a number of dealers. Then you kick the tires and take the car for a test drive. You may return two or three times. Yet a decision about a young law student's career is based on a piece of paper and a meeting! It becomes a matter of sending the right signals.

In essence, every meeting you attend is a prospective job interview and a current job evaluation.

Not long ago I participated in the annual evaluation of the chief executive officer of a public organization on whose board I sit. I'm afraid to say that for most of the board of directors, about 90 percent of their impression of this CEO was literally based on what they saw at our monthly board meetings. Sure, there was some record of performance for the organization, but it's not easy to evaluate a public organization. As far as most of the board members were concerned, the board meetings reflected the health of the organization and the abilities of the CEO. Board members could intellectualize all they wanted about the rest of his performance. The meetings were tangible, real evidence. For the chief executive officer, these board meetings constituted about 5 percent of his whole job, and that's about the priority he gave them. But for board members, the meetings created 90 percent of their perception of him and the organization. From his relative lack of attention to the board meetings, it was clear that the chief executive officer didn't see it that way or understand the consequences.

YOU CAN FOOL SOME OF THE PEOPLE...

In an effort to make the "right impression," some people seem to think that they can get by simply by "giving good meeting": fancy charts and graphs, nice smiles, a fine hello, and a kind good-bye. But while you can fool some of your meeting partners some of the time, you can't generally fool the ones who count. There is a profound difference between those who know how to manage a meeting effectively and what columnist and former newspaper editor Mary Anne Dolan describes as the new school of meeting givers, "executives wielding Cartier briefcases, Montblanc fountain pens, and multicopied agenda documents." These performers substitute *giving good meeting* for *getting something done.* They practice a conscious cynicism toward their meeting partners. But sooner or later a level of meeting is reached where technique is no substitute for task. People who are used to making judgments about others in meetings are also used to seeing people who merely put on a show. They can tell the difference.

BECOMING A MEETING MASTER

If you can recall meetings in which you knew that the other participants just weren't on your level, you can understand the judgments that are made by those with more experience and skills. These people work hard at meetings. Unlike the amateur, they know that a meeting will not achieve its desired goal simply because people with good intentions come together. They respect others who use a meeting well—and they grant responsibility accordingly.

There is no official club of meeting masters. In fact, there are no certain prerequisites. The organization within which you may work, the industry, the type of meeting all set different parameters for what is acceptable, unacceptable, and exceptional meeting behavior. But among top executives there is a level of conduct and understanding that is far more sophisticated than that practiced by the average person. This level of sophistication is practiced by people who may be either well-intentioned or ill-intentioned. They may be genuine and kind or cruel and phony. But they know what they want, and they know how to use the meeting to get it. In your own organization, they are also the persons in the position to affect you and your career, for they view part of their job as making judgments about you.

The top meeting masters rarely use their meeting

skills except to win—that is, to further their purposes in meeting. They think of themselves as leaders and winners. They are neither obvious nor awkward nor foolish. They play under control. They search out other masters the way a coach or superstar sights somebody with good basketball-court sense. They are not showboaters, unless showboating would in a particular instance serve their purpose.

It is important, first of all, for you to recognize—believe—that this level of play exists. Believe it, just as you believe there is a better level of golfer or manager or thinker. Believe it, just as you believe there are those whose meeting skills are not as good as yours. Resist the temptation to think you can do no better. Even the best know they can be better. That's why the superstar shoots 250 three-point shots in practice before the game. That's why meeting masters always watch other masters. Whatever your present level of meeting skills, with an understanding of the rules of the game and experience, you *can* do better.

EACH OF US HAS TO REMIND HIMSELF

Some people begin with an advantage. They may be "better with people," more organized, more confident. But for most of us it is no different than it was for University of California President David Pierpont Gardner, who chaired the successful and influential President's Commission on Excellence in Education. "I wasn't born with my views on meetings," Gardner told me. "I came to them from experience, some positive and some painful. I watched and listened to others who seemed to know what they were doing. I worked at it. I still work at it. Even today I consciously force myself to go through a certain mental checklist with respect to every single meeting I have. Obviously I'm going to recognize and appreciate others who are willing to do the same."

The next meeting you attend, take a good look around you. Ask yourself who appears to be effective in the meeting. Who's participating? See if you can determine who's in command of the material, who is prepared. Which participants seem to be communicating on another level? Who seems to be getting his way? How does he do it? What signals are you sending to the more sophisticated participants? What signals are you sending to the other participants? Attempt to form an overall judgment about the success of the meeting and its members. Rest assured, a judgment is being made about you. If that judgment is positive, it's a career plus. If it is negative, you must learn and apply the meeting strategies that will turn that judgment in your favor.

CHAPTER TWO
Every Meeting Is a Win or a Loss

TIME IS MONEY.

—Ben Franklin

YOU win or lose in every meeting you attend. And as professional baseball club owner Bill Veeck was so fond of saying, winning isn't the most important thing, it's the only thing. But winning doesn't just mean winning the argument. Winning and losing are seldom so obvious in meetings. You can win your point, you can win a raise, and you can win a promotion. You can also win a friend, win a reputation, and put together a winning team. You win when you make the best decision, which may not necessarily be your preconceived one. You win when, early on, you avoid a course of conduct that has no chance of success. You win when you avoid a meeting destined for failure. You win when you bring out the best in an employee or an associate. You sometimes win when you bring out the worst in a rival. You win when you achieve the goal you've set for the meeting.

Winning *is* the only thing, but it's a question first of defining a win. That has to begin with a full recogni-

30

tion of just what each meeting means in terms of costs and benefits, what every meeting does to the participants and the organization beyond the apparent victory or obvious defeat, and all that you risk and forgo simply by choosing to meet.

LEVERAGING YOUR TIME

Thoreau said, "The cost of a thing is the amount of what I will call life which is required to be exchanged for it, immediately or in the long run."

Whenever you attend a meeting you are allocating your time and your life. You have made a judgment that a particular meeting is, in the long run, a more valuable use of your time than anything else you might otherwise do.

Allocation of your time is the most important decision you make for your productivity and success. It's how you manage your business and professional life. You cannot "kill time" in a meeting without doing injury to your life and that of your organization. Thus, *your mere decision to attend a meeting is a win or a loss*, a step forward or a step backward in achieving your basic business and professional goals and the basic goals of the organization.

Moreover, the decision to attend the meeting is a choice about not only the time directly spent in meeting, but also the time spent in preparing (another win or loss) and the time spent in pursuing tasks that are products of the meeting (more wins and losses) as opposed to tasks that are the product of other uses of

31

your time. Therefore, when you think about the time you must commit to any meeting, you must think of it as four or five times greater than the minutes or hours spent in the meeting itself. Every meeting leverages much more of your life and your time.

As a result, meetings are never "neutral." It is never a question of achieving a win or a tie. The mere allocation of your time and energy means that anything resembling a "tie" is always a lost opportunity. And, as we shall see, because there are other unseen consequences to any meeting, a "tie" is a virtual impossibility.

Therefore, when someone in your office asks if you're available for a half-hour meeting this afternoon, don't be fooled. In all likelihood you will be allocating at least two hours of your time and forgoing far more than that one half hour doing something else. When you get that urge to see the boss, remember that you are allocating more than the few minutes it may take. You are allocating time available to spend with him on other issues as well as your time in general. And part of his judgment about you is how you use his time. When someone suggests a business lunch, remember that in all likelihood the cost (and the benefit) will be far greater than the cost of a sandwich and the time it takes to eat it. Every meeting leverages your time, so you must make sure you leverage it wisely.

LEVERAGING THE TIME OF OTHERS

When you call a meeting, particularly when you have the authority to command a meeting and have therefore eliminated individual judgments by other persons about the value of the meeting, you take responsibility for the allocation of their time. That means the leveraging of their time. Merely by calling the meeting, you make a series of separate win/lose judgments regarding everyone's time in the meeting, time preparing for the meeting, and time for pursuing tasks that are generated. While you are certainly capable of prioritizing your own time, you are somewhat less capable in making judgments about other people's time even in pursuit of mutual goals. Obviously these judgments must be made. That's management. But they are also wins or losses—for each individual, for you, and for your organization—of far greater magnitude than you may first assume. A one-hour meeting with four other people may amount to some twenty hours of real, meeting-caused time.

Every meeting leverages time—your time and the time of everyone else who attends. That's why even the decision to meet can be a win/lose situation and can never be made casually.

LEVERAGING COSTS

The simple, direct costs of decisions to meet can readily be seen. For example, your organization may have a policy that business lunches over $50 must be approved in advance; or that there must be preapproval for equipment purchases in excess of $75. Yet your decision to meet for one hour with three other employees whose average salary is $50,000 will cost the organization hundreds of dollars in direct time, thou-

33

sands in premeeting and postmeeting time, and will be approved by no one but you. Whether you have a successful meeting or not, you've spent more company money on this meeting than those expenditures requiring preapproval. These win/lose choices are made every day by most of the people in your organization. Cumulatively, the impact is huge.

Of course this simple analysis of direct costs does not include factoring inefficiency. Estimates center around 50 percent inefficiency for most business meetings. That's still more money. If the inefficient time in meetings were decreased by merely 20 percent, the profits of many companies would be affected considerably. But without yet focusing on efficiency, it is important to keep in mind that all decisions to meet actually cost more money than is generally assumed. Time is money; as time is leveraged, costs are leveraged. It bears repeating to note that a one-hour meeting of four persons will probably cost directly twenty hours of salaried time.

LEVERAGING INDIRECT COSTS

Direct meeting costs are only the tip of the iceberg. Good meetings and bad meetings are contagious. They set a standard for future meetings in which you're involved and for meetings run by other participants when you're not involved. Thus, every meeting leverages the quality of a host of other activities and tasks —hundreds of wins and losses.

How many times have you gone into a meeting still

bothered by a meeting ten minutes earlier? A day in an employee's life can be made or ruined by a single meeting with the boss, affecting his work, his judgment, and his time. Those are losses for the boss and the company as well as the employee. A staff meeting will set the tone for the whole week, creating all sorts of wins and losses for the company. In terms of your business and professional life and the success of your business, organization, or cause, all of these are major wins or losses. Sometimes you won't see the impact of a meeting for days, weeks, or even years. But it will always result in leveraged wins and losses for your organization and for you.

THE MEETING IS OFTEN THE MESSAGE: ANOTHER WIN OR LOSS

A meeting is a medium, and in the famous words of Marshall McLuhan, "the medium is the message." That is, the way we acquire information affects us more than the information itself. A meeting, again in McLuhan's words, "does something to people; it takes hold of them, bumps them around." Thus, the *manner* of a particular meeting can affect the participants and the organization more than the so-called substance.

Years ago, a particular Houston law firm developed the practice of holding a Monday-morning meeting for its eight attorneys. Run by a strong leader, these meetings lasted no more than thirty minutes, often less. Each lawyer shared a brief synopsis of his activities during the coming week. The chair would highlight an

35

opportunity or a problem, but he was always careful to make the meeting a positive, energizing experience. He recognized that what was covered was less important than the feeling he could create. The attorneys nearly shot out of the room, excited about their work and clear about the firm's health and direction. However, a few years later and with a different chair, the Monday-morning meeting had actually become a focal point for firm disharmony. The group was larger, and the meeting had become too long. Some individuals became inattentive, and others used their synopsis time to puff their activities. The new chair, convinced he was dealing with necessary, substantive questions, did not grasp what the meeting was now saying. He focused on "specifics," often questioning calendars and cases. Lawyers became defensive, and the overall tone of the meeting was self-serving and disappointing. The message with which each attorney began his week was now "This is a lousy place full of problems." While particular scheduling conflicts and other issues were resolved at the meeting, the fundamental message had a greater impact, and work suffered.

In every meeting you attend, messages are delivered that have little to do with the presumed purpose. Every meeting teaches. Every meeting talks. People are told whether they are winners or losers, if they are trusted or mistrusted, if the organization is a good or bad place to work. These messages can be far more powerful than any item on the agenda. In fact, you can move through every item on the agenda, win on every issue, and still lose the meeting.

THE BOTTOM LINE

The time commitment for any meeting is greater than the time set aside to meet. The dollar costs are far greater than a pro rata share of participant salaries. The subliminal impact can be far greater than the sum of decisions made and actions taken. When a meeting works, the power—the added value created—is huge. And when the meeting results in poor decisions or unwise actions, failure is leveraged enormously. Thus, your meetings are actually the most dramatic, powerful events in your day. Before you walk into any meeting, before you deal with any substantive issues, you have already begun winning and losing. That is why it is critical to learn the strategies that will make every meeting a win for you.

CHAPTER THREE

Leading or Attending, Make Every Meeting Your Meeting

WHY DON'T YOU SPEAK FOR YOURSELF, JOHN?

—Henry Wadsworth Longfellow
The Courtship of Miles Standish

GIVEN the high stakes in any meeting, the tremendous leverage created, and the judgments made about you, the biggest mistake you can make with any meeting you attend is to abdicate your own responsibility for it. Every meeting steals your time. Every meeting impacts on your professional life and your career. Therefore, *every meeting is your meeting.* You have an obligation to shape it, and to the extent possible you must own every meeting you attend.

"BUT WHAT IF IT'S NOT MY MEETING?"

Just because you didn't "call" the meeting doesn't mean it's not your meeting. Just because you're not chairing the meeting doesn't mean it's not your meeting. And just because your boss is also there doesn't mean it's not your meeting.

The quarterback may call the plays, but it's every bit as much the halfback's football game. Every player has a stake in every meeting. Your role may vary, your control may be circumscribed, you may have no choice but to attend. Still, if you're there, every meeting is your meeting, too.

First of all, of course, you will "call" your share of meetings. Second, you will often have explicit co-ownership of the meeting. Third, in many meetings ownership is up for grabs. To quote Peter Ueberroth, "Authority is 20 percent given and 80 percent taken." Fourth, you have obligations as a "mere" participant (for example, when meeting with your boss) that are often misunderstood or underestimated. Finally, in every meeting you attend, you ought to have your own personal agenda. It may or may not be consistent with the stated agenda of the meeting and may or may not be worth the risk in pursuing. But at minimum, you've got to consider it.

WHEN YOU CALL THE MEETING

It is generally accepted that when you call a meeting you take responsibility for it. It's "your" meeting. You're going to be perceived as the one to bear the burden of responsibility for its success or failure. You will need to share that burden without losing control of "your" meeting. And most people will defer to you —often carelessly. But you are also going to have to be on the lookout for meeting masters with conflicting agendas who may have no intention of permitting you sole ownership—and they're right!

CO-OWNERSHIP

A business associate might suggest that you and he have lunch next Tuesday. You say, "Yes, sounds great." He has proposed the lunch meeting, but by saying yes, you've made the meeting your meeting, too. You now have co-ownership and responsibility for the success or failure of that business lunch.

Suppose you don't know why your associate suggested the lunch. But if you don't have any idea why you're having a business lunch, why would you forgo another use of that time? The truth is that you've probably got some sort of implicit agenda in mind: maintaining relations, getting information, you're open to new deals—whatever. That vague notion of an agenda makes it your meeting. Your focus on that lunch should be first to clarify and then to facilitate that vague agenda.

Screenwriters often call Norman Lear, the producer and creator of such megahits as *All in the Family* and *Maude*, to pitch story ideas. Let's say that through a friend you're able to schedule a meeting with Lear to pitch your story idea. Your meeting. But does Lear have any less of a responsibility? Isn't it his meeting, too?

"My responsibility," says Lear, "is to encourage or allow, as the case may be, the best-possible presentation of your idea. I really want a successful presentation, not a trial. I want a clear look at that idea. I may not like the idea after getting a clear look, but I want that clear look, and I structure the meeting accordingly. That's my responsibility, and I take it seriously. I can't just sit there passively. In the end, I'm the one who's got to make a decision, not you."

Whose meeting is it, then?

"Well, it has to be my meeting as much as it is yours," says Lear.

In fact, the meeting between Lear and you is almost two different meetings, given the different perspectives of the meeting partners. The meeting you want is the one whose goal is to *sell* Norman Lear your idea, however you do it. His meeting is the one whose purpose is to *get a clear look* at a story idea so that he can decide whether or not to buy it. These are different goals, nearly different meetings. Which meeting are you going to attend? You're going to have to be prepared for both. But in the end, you will want it to have been your meeting. That is, you're not seeking to offer a "clear look." You're seeking a sale.

Thus, to a greater or lesser extent, depending upon the circumstances, your assent to any meeting "called" by someone else makes you, too, responsible and gives you ownership of the meeting. It's your meeting.

Whose meeting is the one composed of five equally ranked staff members whom the boss asks to solve a problem? If the group asks Bill to act as leader, is it now all of a sudden just his meeting? Of course not. It's certainly an opportunity for Bill to control the meeting; he's got a bigger role. But the rest of the group can't forgo responsibility for the meeting simply because Bill is the chair.

Whose meeting is the monthly meeting of the board

41

of directors? Some would say it belongs to the chair or chief executive officer because he or she is responsible for preparing the agenda and wielding the gavel. But does that mean his ownership interest dissolves if he passes the gavel to a committee chair? Of course not. And what about the member who wants an important project to receive board approval? Certainly, to the extent that any part of the meeting may impact upon that project, it's also his meeting. In fact, every single board member has a fiduciary responsibility to the company and thereby some ownership of and responsibility for the meeting.

The next time someone suggests a meeting and you're not sure why, before you say yes ask, "What do you have in mind?" Then make sure you're clear why you're there. You have responsibility for your career and for your company or organization. You are forgoing other opportunities, and that makes any meeting you agree to attend your meeting, too.

THE BATTLE FOR CONTROL

Sometimes, ownership of a meeting is up for grabs.

When I first joined my law firm as a young associate just out of law school, I learned very quickly that merely because I asked for a meeting did not necessarily mean it would be "my" meeting. I made an appointment to see one of the senior partners with whom I was working on a number of corporate matters. One of those matters involved preparation for a shareholders meeting in San Francisco. I had never attended a shareholders meeting, and although there was another, more senior lawyer working on the matter who would have to accompany the senior partner to San Francisco, I wanted to ask the senior partner if I could attend. That was my goal in asking for the meeting.

I came out of that meeting with a strong "maybe" on going to the shareholders meeting. I also came out having taken on two additional work assignments, having accepted a request that I attend a charity dinner that evening (someone had canceled at the senior partner's table, and he needed a replacement), and having volunteered (I really did!) to do a draft of a speech he was to give to a local Chamber of Commerce.

I didn't know what had hit me. All I had done was schedule a meeting. But once that meeting was set, the senior partner had quite properly developed his own objectives and agenda. We spent nine-tenths of the meeting on *his* agenda and one-tenth on *my* agenda. It became far more his meeting than mine. And I was the one who had asked to meet.

As someone who calls a meeting, you always risk losing "your" meeting to a participant, particularly those experienced in the management of meetings. Thus, if you call or attend a meeting without a strategic sense of where you're going and a knowledge of the techniques to get you there, you're liable to end up someplace you'd rather not be.

Obligations as "Mere" Participant

"A wise meeting attendee will ask the chair what he wants to get done and how to help," says former Assistant Secretary of State and chief hostage negotiator Warren Christopher. By attending the meeting, or by having placed yourself in a position (as an employee) that requires your attendance, you have made the meeting goal your goal. Again, that makes the meeting your meeting, not merely the leader's.

Let's say your boss calls you in for a no-advanced-warning meeting at 3:00 P.M. His meeting? Even before you go in you should be asking, "What could he want, and how can I help him achieve it?" Once you get there he asks you to give him a detailed briefing on a complicated program under your supervision. For the next thirty minutes it's suddenly your meeting, a meeting (in this case a presentation) within a meeting.

When a superior calls the meeting, your primary interest is usually going to be the same as his interest. But it's still your interest. Although you and your superior have different roles, you have a mutuality of interests. He's the boss, but if he says something that is contrary to his (and your) interest, are you going to ignore it? You shouldn't. The "yes-man" is a yes-man largely because he confuses mutual, fundamental interests with merely pleasing the boss at the moment. As Don Gevirtz, the Foothill Group chairman, told me, "I wish more of my employees would maintain a greater sense of what we're trying to accomplish in the meetings we have. I'm trying to maintain an objective, but I'm not perfect. I wish they would take as much responsibility for keeping us on track as I have to. If they did, we'd get more done a lot faster. Instead, they put the whole burden on me. They're more interested in saying what they think I want to hear at a given moment than achieving the goal—our goal—for the meeting."

Therefore, begin to see yourself as "owning" the meeting with your boss, not to undermine it, but to maintain and achieve a mutual objective.

PERSONAL OBJECTIVES

In every meeting you attend, you have—or you should have—a personal objective or objectives. That personal objective may be exactly the same as the stated objective of the meeting. Or it may not. To the extent that it's exactly the same as the stated objective, it simply reinforces your obligation to help achieve the objective as well as your responsibility for the meeting.

To the extent that the stated objective of the meeting is not exactly your objective, you have a more difficult situation. You must weigh your objective against the stated objective and make choices. Your interest may be only marginally different, or it could be totally against the stated objective. In either case, from your perspective (just as in the meeting with Norman Lear), you're attending a somewhat different meeting from that attended by each of your meeting partners. The meeting involving your personal goals and interests is your own meeting. You're the only one fully capable of understanding and balancing your interests. To the extent your interests conflict with the stated objective and the objectives of other participants, and to the extent you decide that those conflicts really do matter, you've got to own any part of the meeting that affects you and your interests.

Let's assume that your company is in the process of redetermining the most efficient organizational structure. The more efficient the organization, the better the company does and, presumably, the better you do. But let's also assume that what might be arguably the most efficient structure will place you under a superior who is going nowhere, and you are certain this will adversely affect your advancement within the company. A meeting has been called to assess three alternative structures. Now, it may be that the structure that places you in jeopardy is clearly so much more efficient that you have no alternative but to support it. But if that structure is only marginally better, you've got a tougher choice. And if it's really a toss-up, you owe it to yourself to move that meeting toward the decision that benefits you personally. You've got a very particular ownership interest in that meeting. To that extent, you've got to approach the meeting as your meeting.

Personal agendas can destroy meetings. But they exist and are quite defensible at times. If someone in the organization is out to get your job, you may have to assert ownership over a meeting to protect yourself. You must carefully weigh your personal interests, but you can never ignore them. To understand the consequences and make the assessment, you must begin by seeing every meeting as potentially your meeting.

MEETINGS WITHIN MEETINGS

There are *at least* as many potential objectives for a meeting as the sum of the potential relations among the meeting members. Each member has personal objectives for the meeting. But in addition, each member can have an explicit or implicit objective to achieve with *each other meeting partner.* Your objective with one or more of these people may be more important to you than the stated objective of the meeting.

A friend of mine once asked another acquaintance, as a personal favor, to serve on a committee he chaired. Only as a personal favor, the acquaintance agreed to do so. But at the committee meetings he came to disagree with nearly everything the chair did. Not only did the acquaintance waste his own time at the meeting (since he had no real interest in the subject matter), but he lost sight of the real objective of his participation: to please a friend. His interaction vis-à-vis his friend was the meeting that mattered, not the meeting as a whole.

Conflicting personal objectives with meeting partners can undermine a meeting. But they almost always exist and are another reason you will want to own a part of any meeting you attend.

SHOWBOATING

What about the guy who's always taking control of a meeting by showboating or knocking others? Of course, you shouldn't do this, let alone *appear* to be putting your interests above the basic interests of the meeting. In the long run, that's not serving your own interests. There's no quicker way to undermine yourself as well as the meeting. If you get any hint that this is something of which you're guilty, or if that's the way you come across, you're probably defeating rather than achieving your personal objectives.

There's another issue to consider when dealing with the control-oriented person. "The showboater always seeking control tells me two things," says Ron Rogers, president of Rogers & Associates, a public relations firm that represents Suzuki and Philip Morris, among others. "First, it's poor judgment on his part, since I'm not going to appreciate such behavior to the extent it undermines the meeting, me, or my other employees. Second, it may be my fault and my management problem. If I've allowed the meeting to be controlled by someone else, or if I've created incentives or conditions that encourage behavior inconsistent with my own goals for the meeting, I've got to reconsider how I'm handling the meeting. But on the other hand, it's possible that with a little guidance the abilities that allow him to control the meeting, if positively channeled, may make him president of the company someday."

TAKING RESPONSIBILITY

When the stakes are so high, when you risk so much in the way of time, energy, employees, profits and programs, when there are those who seek victories over you, when you are judged and advanced on your ability to handle each meeting whether as leader or participant, when you really do have an ownership interest in every meeting you attend, the real problem with meetings is that we don't take them seriously enough. Not solemnly, but seriously.

Too many people treat meetings as time fillers or events of little consequence. "What are you doing this afternoon?" "Oh, nothing much, just a meeting. . . ." Or "If I can get through this awful meeting, I can get some real work done." As a result, their meetings are of little consequence. Too many people swear that they hate meetings—"Oh, God, not another meeting!"—only to worsen them by refusing to prepare or focus. Too many of us get trapped—"What am I doing in this meeting?" Others act as if merely *holding* the meeting is what their work is about. They are the René Descartes of meetings: "I meet, therefore I am." Hence, perhaps, the awful phrase "to take a meeting," as if it were akin to taking a shower: just stand there, and warm results will wash over you.

Too many people wrongly presume that someone else has all responsibility for the meeting and for the information and expertise underlying any actions taken—a form of collective surrender to the meeting. Under these circumstances, we should be prepared for the consequences: failed meetings.

You should be different. The meeting master doesn't profess to hate all meetings, only poor meetings, so he makes certain that *all* his meetings are effective. The meeting master does not confuse the appearance of action with action, although he may utilize appearance

49

to further action. He takes responsibility because he knows it's always his life, his time, his money, his purpose, and his career at stake. He knows he has a different role in different meetings, but he also knows *it is always his meeting.* Ultimately, he knows he must encourage others to take more responsibility, too.

Learn to take responsibility for every meeting, whether you're leading or attending. If you do, you'll actually find yourself going to fewer and better meetings, for you'll quickly learn to be more specific about what you want to accomplish, and you'll be far more willing to do all that may be required to achieve a win for yourself, your company, or your cause.

It may seem like a lot of work, but taking responsibility for every meeting is a great deal easier once you realize what you risk by abdicating responsibility. The consequences of failing to take responsibility are far worse. With so much on the line, no matter who is formally in control, whether you're the boss or the employee, whether you're the chair or one of the participants, you must begin by seeing every meeting as *your* meeting. It is around that perception that all the other meeting strategies revolve.

Part Two

WISE MEN/
FOOLISH MEETINGS

The fool doth think he is wise, but the
wise man knows himself to be a fool.

—SHAKESPEARE
As You Like It

CHAPTER FOUR

Understanding the Psychology of Meetings

FILL A THEATRE WITH A THOUSAND RENANS AND A THOUSAND HERBERT SPENCERS, AND THE COMBINATION OF THOSE TWO THOUSAND BRAINS OF GENIUS WILL PRODUCE ONLY THE SOUL OF A CONCIERGE.

—Octave Uzanne

THERE is a tendency for every meeting to drift toward collective incompetence. "Groups of individuals are far more likely to err than individuals," wrote English author and statesman T. B. Macaulay. "Groups give reign to instincts which individuals acting alone are forced to keep in check." Years ago, German writer and theorist Friedrich Schiller put it this way: Anyone taken as an individual is tolerably sensible and reasonable, but as a member of a crowd he at once becomes a blockhead. As one business executive stated recently, "Smart people just seem to leave part of their judgment at the door when they go into a meeting." I call this tendency the "phenomenon of collective incompetence," wherein very wise individuals can still compose very foolish groups. It is important to understand this tendency and its causes in order to develop effective meeting strategies.

People meet because common, rational interests bring them together. However, these presumed interests, often poorly articulated, are easily overwhelmed by conflicting personal needs and interests, emotions, difficulties of communication, the tendency to abdicate responsibility, and the strange dynamics of group behavior. As a result, not only does an individual meeting participant act differently in a meeting than he would on his own, or differently in a group of seven than in an encounter with another single person, but also the group qua group develops its own memory, personality, and judgment. Therefore, whether a meeting comprises two or two thousand, it is important to remember that *all assemblages of men are different from the men themselves.* And whether it is a simple employee staff meeting, the management committee of an accounting firm or law firm, or an academic committee, all assemblages will tend to drift toward collective incompetence. Properly managed, a meeting can achieve extraordinary results, but just as often decisions made and actions taken by a group of persons are likely to be less competent than those made or taken by the very same individuals acting alone. Or, in the words of Samuel Johnson, "Get together a hundred men or two men, however sensible they may be, and you are very likely to have a mob."

This means that contrary to popular practice, you cannot afford to view meetings as likely in and of themselves to culminate in positive results without a great deal of work. In fact, you should reverse the presumption. As George Herbert wrote, "Every man hath a fool in one sleeve," and he is encouraged to appear in meetings. Meetings are inherently risky enterprises, mobs in waiting, more susceptible to passions, pieties, persuasion, and manipulation of all kinds and degrees than are the individuals who participate in them. Taken another way, a meeting begins with the same risk of injury as a motor vehicle containing a steering mechanism at each passenger seat.

THE PREVALENCE OF COLLECTIVE INCOMPETENCE

This phenomenon of collective incompetence is not limited to the local school board or the lower levels of business. It reaches into the highest levels of government, business, and the professions. Victor Palmieri, president of the Palmieri Company and a highly regarded corporate workout specialist, notes, for example, that whenever he has come in to study a troubled company—Penn Central Railroad, Chrysler, Baldwin United—he has been "most of all struck by the amazing contrast between the individual background, experience, and general abilities of the board members and the collective stupidity of the board. And it's not just business groups. It happens with all groups, particularly in times of crisis—this tendency of the group to react in crazy ways that the individuals would not."

The problem in getting a group to function effectively was recognized long ago in Charles Kettering's famous line, "If you want to kill any idea in the world, get a committee working on it." But the inherent difficulties confront all meetings. The weekly staff meeting with the long agenda seems to produce few results, and the same matters appear again and again for discussion. The meeting to pick a particular new computer plan actually becomes a rehash of whether a new system is even necessary. You think you've clearly delegated assignments to subordinates, only to find them saying, "No one told me." You find yourself in meeting after meeting saying, "What am I doing in this meeting?" And you get out of a meeting shaking your head, surprised and amazed at what was decided.

The fact that meetings tend to drift toward collective incompetence should not be a surprise. Would it surprise you if a vehicle operated concurrently by four different drivers took considerable time to get anywhere or intermittently headed in different directions? Of course not. It would be more surprising if such a vehicle actually arrived somewhere close to an agreed destination in only somewhat more time than originally anticipated.

But once you recognize that all meetings leverage time and money, wins and losses, and that the natural drift is toward losses, your basic attitude toward any meeting must change. If you can begin with a recognition of the inherent limitations of meetings in general and yet—as we shall see—maintain respect and appreciation for both the process and the particular individuals in attendance, you will be on the road to successful meetings.

While collective incompetence is not inevitable, the tendency toward bizarre group action by otherwise competent participants is always present. Meeting masters manipulate the sources of collective incompetence to achieve certain goals. When the goal is group wisdom, the master does all he can to eliminate potential sources of collective incompetence. When his goal is different from the stated group goal, he may choose to stimulate sources of collective incompetence in order to undermine an intended course of action. "For example," a well-known executive told me, "committees have enough problems on their own. When I want a committee to succeed, I try to appoint the most competent and most widely respected person to chair it. I give it a grand title. It gives the meeting standing. That helps. But when I want it to fail, I might make sure the committee has at least one 'abominable no-man,' someone whose interminable negativity will confuse and derail group thinking and further tend to prevent any reasonable action. Or I put people on the committee whom I know just don't get along. That always fouls things up a bit."

But no one has to be malicious for collective incompetence to take its course; it will do so on its own unless meeting participants recognize in advance the sources that contribute to the tendency and how to fight them. First among these is an understanding of how people in groups usually think and act.

UNDERSTANDING THE GROUP MIND

At the heart of both collective genius and collective incompetence is the "group mind." Psychologists believe that groups of persons meeting together actually

57

form a group mind or group memory that facilitates group thought and collective action. This enlarged mind has a tremendous capacity to achieve effective results, but it also has severe limitations.

When a group of people meet, more is going on than a series of voices or votes that reflect how the individuals think. The individual minds interact and influence each other. Out of the exchanges the group expresses information, goals, solutions, and decisions. Particular thoughts may be expressed by individuals, but these thoughts are as much the product of the group and its chain of thinking as the creation of any one person. In this sense, the whole has far greater capacity than the sum of the parts. Along with other goals, it is this collective wisdom that we often seek in meetings. Its value is not only the collective knowledge of the participants, but also the additional knowledge, wisdom, or creativity—added value—born of the mix of dynamic elements within the group.

Crucial to the functioning of the group mind is a "group memory," a common language and a common set of presumptions. Individual expertise cannot be shared and the whole cannot "think" without certain common foundations. Every meeting group brings to the table separate, distinct perspectives of all of the individuals within the group, but there must be a common memory composed of information and experience shared as a group in order to reach group decisions.

Notwithstanding the potential genius of the group mind, because individuals bring such different perspectives to the table, communication in meetings is much more confused than we tend to think. In fact, group thought is extremely difficult. Witness the following exchange:

> Bill (chairing the meeting):
> "We're here to discuss the location of the new plant. The alternatives are Pittsburgh, Cleveland, or St. Louis."
>
> John (losing his influence in the company):
> "I still don't think we need a new plant."
>
> Sarah (responsible for production):
> "We already decided that question. But I still think one plant won't be enough to meet our production needs."
>
> Pete (the comptroller, looking gravely at documents reflecting past estimates, but in agreement that a new plant is needed):
> "You're wrong. We've consistently overestimated production."
>
> Sarah: "But we've always met any demand by our distributors."
>
> John: "We're just not as efficient as our competitors. They outproduce us. If we were more efficient, we'd actually have too much product. I don't see why we need another plant."
>
> Sarah: "The problem isn't productivity, it's wages. We have to pay higher wages than our competitors, so the product costs more."
>
> Pete (again referring to the statistics):
> "She's right. Our wages are higher."

Bill: "Look, we've been through all that before. We decided we need a new plant. Is it Pittsburgh, Cleveland, or St. Louis?"

Alan (the compromiser):
"Well, where are we likely to contract for the lowest wages?"

Pete (referring to statistics):
"Pittsburgh has the lowest average per capita income of the three cities."

Alan: "I think we need to pay attention to wages. I vote for Pittsburgh."

Bill: "Everyone agreed? Okay."

John: "I just want to go on record as saying this is a bad idea."

Obviously, this is a hypothetical and oversimplified example. But it reflects many a group discussion. Individuals respond to statements by other individuals, whether relevant or not. The group records statements in its memory, often in error. And the final decision is a compromise based on inaccurate or misleading information. In this case, among other problems, in arguing for the development of a new factory, Pete has used the wrong statistics about Pittsburgh. Nonetheless, his "fact" has been assimilated by the group unchallenged. It is now part of the group memory and was implicit in its final, flawed decision.

LIMITATIONS OF THE GROUP MIND

Researchers have also learned that there are certain things the human mind does very poorly. For example, Nobel Laureate Herbert Simon, in studying the human mind and computers, has found that the most that human beings can hold in short-term memory without forgetting something is six or seven pieces of data. A group of people, therefore, will remember information differently, as well as forget. Some miscommunication, some misunderstanding, is *inevitable* in any meeting. Moving a group of minds toward the solution of a problem or toward acceptance of your point of view requires the ability to lead different minds, as well as the group mind, along the same journey to the goal. When viewed this way, it's a very difficult undertaking. If you are meeting with someone who is intent on defeating your purpose, or who simply disagrees, it is harder still.

Remember the game you played as a child when you whispered a story one by one among a group of your classmates? When the last child told the story to the teacher, it had changed totally. Each child heard the story in a different way and then told it differently. And this was when everyone *wanted* to tell the same simple story.

In adult meetings, you are dealing not only with memory, but with power, ego, emotions, ambitions, hidden motivations, and a host of other factors. These factors may be more powerful than any logic, and as we have seen, even the information received and re-corded by the group may be flawed, impairing the logic as well.

COMMON TENDENCIES OF THE GROUP MIND

COGNITIVE DISSONANCE

People dislike inconsistency and will attempt to elimi-nate it. Cognitive dissonance is the mental conflict that occurs when beliefs or assumptions are contra-dicted by new information. The unease or tension that the conflict arouses in a person is relieved by one of several defensive maneuvers. The person rejects, ex-plains away, or avoids the new information. He may convince himself that no conflict really exists and thus reconcile differences. In a group, when informa-tion challenges group beliefs, such reactions can be fast and furious. In a single moment the group can react to preserve its preconceptions and a stampede develops for or against an idea.

DISASSOCIATION FROM THE TASK

Because group thinking can be so difficult, individuals actually tend to disassociate from the task. This is done in a number of ways. For example, Mary may believe the rest of the group is more informed than she is. She drops out of the discussion when she disagrees, but wanting to remain accepted, she votes for the pro-posal anyway. John may simply daydream. Or, very commonly, the mechanical task may replace the substantive task as the focus of attention. For example, a substantive proposal is presented with charts and graphs. The group critiques the charts and graphs instead of the proposal.

LOWEST COMMON DENOMINATOR AND HIGHEST RISK

The most common response of the group mind appears to be to find a consensus based on the lowest common denominator. To reach a conclusion on the stated task, the group is forced to agree in order to avoid division. The result is a compromise that may not solve the problem but does salve feelings and egos.

However, the fact that groups are hostile to that which is divisive does not necessarily mean they will *always* take a conservative, narrow path. In fact, groups may arrive at riskier decisions than individuals do alone, particularly committees of subordinates. In a 1967 paper, psychologists N. Kogan and M. A. Wallach identified what has become known as the "risky shift effect": decisions by individuals, on their own, are more conservative than those made by the individuals when acting together. Kogan and Wallach attributed this to the diffusion of responsibility among group members. Others have said that individuals who are prone to risks seem also to dominate meetings.

GET OUT OF THE ROOM!

There are also, in fact, psychological and physiological explanations for certain kinds of individual behavior in group situations. Doctors David Charney and

William Anixter practice psychiatry and specialize in the treatment of anxiety. They note that the most common malady, ahead of substance abuse and depression, is the individual's fear of groups, which affects to some degree 40 percent of the public. In response to such fears, the body produces higher amounts of adrenaline. The increased adrenaline alters the individual's perception of himself and skews his expectations of what can reasonably be accomplished. He is likely, as a result, to expect more from the meeting than can reasonably be accomplished and to make judgments in a meeting he would not make on his own.

Convinced that it really is a matter of body chemistry, Victor Palmieri offers an only partially facetious cure: "There is a change in body chemistry, a drop in acuity to the lowest common level of stupidity, so when you see confusion in a meeting the important thing is to get out of the room as quickly as you can before your body chemistry changes!"

Whether you get high risk or low gain, for our purposes it is enough to remember that, in any meeting you attend, the participants think less clearly as a group than the sum of the intelligence would suggest and less clearly than any single member may recognize at any particular moment. The dynamics of the group mind are different from the dynamics of the individual mind. Whether it's a staff meeting or an intense negotiation, group members tend to disassociate from the real task and move toward levels of abstraction. But you don't have to leave the room. You have to refocus the group and continually limit the sources of collective incompetence.

Sources of Collective Incompetence

In order to meet your goal for any meeting, you're going to have to be conscious of the sources that often impair group thinking and encourage collective incompetence.

MISCOMMUNICATION

Individuals come to a meeting with different abilities, experience, intelligence, language, and communicative styles. Furthermore, they communicate with more than the spoken word. Body language, clothing, and personality all say things to meeting partners. Some miscommunication is inevitable, and there is a continual need for clarification.

OUTSIDE PRESSURES

A meeting is often the focal point for decisions made elsewhere. Thus the actions within a meeting may affect its outcome far less than the pressures brought to bear on the participants from outside. For example, the value of any idea debated by the members of a city council may be much less important than the pressures and forces that weigh on council members from outside the meeting, the most important question being "How does this affect me and my supporters?" But the political process is only the most obvious example. In all meetings external factors are important.

Joe's argument against the new computer system may have nothing to do with the computer system but may reflect a relationship with a competitor. No one representing labor or management would enter discussions without an understanding not only of the stated positions of the other side, but also of the relationship to and standing of the representative to his "client." Does he have power? Is his job in jeopardy? What are his problems?

Whatever the pressures may be, they cloud the apparent discussion and alter the meaning of everything said. Nevertheless, participants will respond to the literal statements. You cannot remove these influences, you can only deal with them. The tendency is for participants to presume that the aspirations of meeting partners are clear. Reverse your presumption. Ask yourself what pressures weigh on your prospective meeting partners. Only then can you choose whether and how to deal with them.

DIFFERENT AGENDA

Every individual comes into the meeting with his or her own personal agenda to accomplish. Jonathan knocks Sid's proposal because Sid criticized his proposal last week. Karen wants Al's job. What any meeting leader wants, of course, is to have a meeting wherein personal agendas are as consistent as possible with the stated agenda of the meeting. But this is not always possible. You may choose not to tolerate actions at a staff meeting that are the product of a personal agenda, but it is folly not to recognize that such an agenda does exist. And, in many forms of meeting, personal agendas are very appropriate. Don't presume that the personal agenda is the same as the stated agenda for the meeting. Ask yourself what's behind a criticism or suggestion.

INSECURITIES AND BASIC HUMAN NEEDS

How often have you sat through a meeting in which many or even a majority of the participants implicitly agree on what may be wrong with a policy, or a meeting in which policy is developed—including the corrective steps required—and yet no one moves to correct the problem?

We tend to go mad in herds, but we tend to recover our senses one by one. To suggest change or to question, one must first speak as an individual, expose oneself. Was I listening? Did I miss something? Is it just me? Fearful of being seen as stupid, malcontent, or ungrateful, we tend to go along with whatever the group decides. In some cases we may be worried about being ostracized; we want to be liked; we don't want to delay the meeting. In other cases we may be concerned about being fired or jeopardizing a promotion. Individuals recover their direction one by one and fail to confront what they perceive as the majority view. Don't presume understanding and accord merely because no one speaks (unless, of course, you simply want to ram a point through). At nearly all times there are differences of opinion around the table.

The most powerful interests in any meeting, far more powerful than the purported purpose of the meeting itself, are the basic human needs of the participants. These include economic well-being, a sense of belonging, the need for recognition, and control of one's life. These needs are expressed at nearly every point in a meeting whether or not a participant gives them direct voice. Recognizing that, you can appeal to these interests quite apart from the purpose of the meeting and thereby undermine or support the stated agenda.

PERSONAL FEELINGS

A close friend of mine and his fellow employees work for a boss who calls staff meetings at the drop of a hat. To a person they have always believed the meetings too long, too numerous, and most often unnecessary. But they have not been able to bring themselves to tell the boss. Now, after the passage of time, the pattern of these meetings is so ingrained that they are virtually incapable of confronting the problems that really exist. Personal feelings about fellow participants, or about the meeting itself, will always distort comments in the meeting and undermine collective thinking.

COMPETITION

A meeting provides a forum for assessing and expressing status within the group, and that will affect the behavior of group members. Employees will always alter behavior around the boss, for example. The result is that what is said may be unrelated to the common objective. Staff persons will both intentionally and unintentionally play games with one another in meetings in order to achieve recognition or define territory. Peers will look for ego reinforcement. Some of these shenanigans are quickly seen, but others are more subtle. Accept the fact that they are probably going on to some extent in any meeting.

DISTRACTIONS

Every meeting will have distractions, from the late arrivals and the early departures, to uncomfortable surroundings, to telephone interruptions, poor technical facilities—you name it. No matter how much you plan, it is likely that some distractions will occur, making it all the more difficult to focus the attention of meeting participants. Some people intentionally create distractions to get the group going in another direction. Even when there are few outside distractions, all participants tend to wander from time to time. The result is a short circuit of the group mind. Sometimes individual minds are turned off to doodle, to daydream, to think about another meeting; sometimes the whole group is interrupted by an outside distraction—a dispute that erupts between members, or perhaps even the air conditioning. Whatever it is, the group mind is not always playing the same game. As the meeting moves along, you may not realize you've lost members and the group mind as a whole. You must presume that you are losing some of the members all of the time.

THOUGHT DISPLACEMENT AND BUZZ WORDS

Thought displacement is a particular form of distraction. It can strike at any time. A line of thought is being pursued when suddenly a "buzz word" exploding with different meanings takes the conversation in a completely different direction. Or a glib participant, in midargument, adds two and two and gets five, but nobody notices. All of a sudden the car is careening out of control.

Thought displacement can be intentional or unintentional. Either way, it derails the meeting. I don't believe a meeting of three or more people can occur in which thought displacement does not take place *at least* once or twice. It goes with the territory. You must presume it is happening throughout the meeting.

THE LAW OF TRIVIALITY AND THE LAW OF AVOIDANCE

"The time spent on any item of the agenda will be in inverse proportion to the sum involved," opined Professor Parkinson. Furthermore, the time spent will be in inverse proportion to the complexity or difficulty of the issue: the law of avoidance.

Each year a particular accounting firm adopts its annual budget, which at this point has become relatively substantial. Certainly much time has already been spent by the staff when the matter comes before the management committee for approval. Still, it is extraordinary that this multimillion-dollar budget is approved almost without comment. At the same time, a party for the firm's summer interns may take two hours of discussion by the same eight accountants.

The board of directors of another company recently had before it for approval the acquisition of a new information system for the organization. Fully implemented, the system would cost about $15 million. A 120-page proposal drafted by staff had been distributed prior to the meeting. A staff presentation was made at the meeting. The board members asked only two questions: "Can I plug in my home computer to this system?" and "When will it be in place?" The $15 million purchase was approved without further discussion. The next item on the agenda, picking the locations for the next years' meetings, then took one hour and fifteen minutes.

Complex matters—irrespective of money—*tend* to be ignored, and simple matters *tend* to be belabored. People are simply more comfortable discussing what they know rather than what they don't know. And most people want to demonstrate what they know rather than struggle with what they don't know. This means that the group avoids the tough questions and concentrates on the easy ones; they will avoid the real issues and look for the phony, comfortable ones, dragging the meeting toward contented failure. Expect this tendency in all your meetings.

PERSONALITIES AND ROLES

Some personalities simply don't mix. Some relationships carry limitations. Personal and professional feelings will further distort communication. In addition, it has been shown that irrespective of personalities, individuals naturally take on certain roles depending upon other participants: the facilitator, the disrupter, the complainer, and so on. This role playing can sometimes be helpful. It can be harmful if perceived for more than it is. Nearly everyone adopts a role of some kind during a meeting. Nearly everyone harbors feelings about the other participants.

INCOMPETENT MEMBERS AND THE LOWEST COMMON DENOMINATOR

An incompetent or destructive participant, like the "abominable no-man," tends to bring the whole group to his level. Even if everyone else does his best to assist in achieving the meeting's goal, avoid personal agendas and buzz words, and focus on the real issues, a single participant can derail the meeting. He forces others to respond to peripheral issues and encourages disassociation from the task. Fear of hurting his feelings and disrupting the group further, and reverence for democracy may allow him to take the meeting's steering wheel and drive where he must. The group tends to defer, dropping to the lowest common denominator.

WHAT THE PHENOMENON OF COLLECTIVE INCOMPETENCE MEANS FOR YOU

The sources of collective incompetence reside in all meetings. Good intentions alone are no match. It is of no use to cast blame. But it takes far more work to accomplish your meeting goal than many people think. When considering any meeting, when developing your strategy, remember that all of these problems are in your way. Remember also that you are seeking a bigger win and risking a bigger loss than you may have first imagined. Before you call or attend a meeting, ask yourself: Is there any other way? For what may seem like an easy task is really fraught with inherent difficulty. If there is no other way, you must be aware of the many complex psychological forces that will encourage the meeting to drift toward collective incompetence and failure. By understanding these forces and how they are likely to manifest themselves during the meeting, you can devise the strategies that will make them work for—not against—you.

CHAPTER FIVE

Control Is Not a Dirty Word

MEN FUNDAMENTALLY CAN NO MORE GET ALONG
WITHOUT DIRECTION THAN THEY CAN WITHOUT
EATING, DRINKING, AND SLEEPING.

—Charles de Gaulle

IN essence, in every meeting you lead or attend, if you
are not openly battling a foe, you are battling to keep
irrelevant issues, inconsistent interests, personal
needs, and distractions from derailing the meeting.
And you are battling with the more negative dynamics
of group behavior. These are risks that go with any
meeting. At the same time, you are seeking to harness
the wonderful power of the group mind and leverage
your positive influence as a manager. To get the most
out of a meeting, you must limit the risks and focus
the group to achieve your purpose. You must therefore
(1) limit the number and kinds of tasks to be undertaken; (2) limit the number of participants; (3) spend
more time in preparation and less time in meeting;
and (4) ensure that the meeting environment is consistent with your purpose and the tasks to be performed.
These points apply to *any* meeting, whether the
number of people attending is two or two thousand.

LIMITING THE NUMBER AND KINDS OF TASKS

Meetings tend to fail in direct proportion to the number and variety of tasks being undertaken. The more narrow the defined task, the better the group does and the better you will do. Certain groups, by their makeup, are appropriate for only certain tasks. In addition, the more issues, the more tasks undertaken in the same meeting, the more difficulty in "thinking" successfully. Getting the group to think is already difficult. Reduce the issues and tasks to the smallest number possible within the expertise of the participants, and make clear exactly what the task is.

LIMIT THE NUMBER OF PARTICIPANTS

Meetings tend to fail in direct proportion to the number of people actively participating. Each additional person brings his component of basic needs, competitiveness, aspirations, agenda, personality, and feelings (as well as talent and abilities) to the meeting. Moreover, with each person added to the meeting, the number of relationships among members increases geometrically. When three people meet, the dynamics are A vs. B, A vs. C, and B vs. C, or three sets of relationships. But four people meeting creates seven sets of relationships among the participants. A ten-person meeting actually creates forty-five different relationships. As a meeting grows in size, productivity decreases dramatically. Each additional person increases the risk of failure. So each person's participation in the meeting must be fully justified. As a general rule, seek to reduce the size of all meetings.

PREPARE MORE AND MEET LESS

Meetings tend to fail in inverse proportion to preparation and time and in direct proportion to meeting time. The most important work for any meeting is done prior to the meeting. Once the meeting begins, options for leadership are severely constrained. More time should be spent in preparation and consultation. In addition, the attention span of the average person in a meeting falls substantially after about one hour. Make your meeting as short as possible. Ironically, you do this by preparing more.

ESTABLISH A MEETING ENVIRONMENT CONSISTENT WITH YOUR PURPOSE AND THE TASKS TO BE PERFORMED

Meetings fail when the environment is inconsistent with the purpose. Everything possible should be done so that the environment for the meeting by its nature encourages attention to the particular task. Too often the environment and task are inconsistent. For instance, if you're brainstorming, ideas will be scarce in an authoritarian environment. This means matching the desired task with the proper location, seating, and timing as well as the appropriate participants.

CONTROLLING THE PROCESS

The way you limit risks in any meeting is by controlling the process. That means controlling the decision whether or not to meet, the number and kinds of people you bring into the meeting, the number and kinds of activities sought from the group, the length of time devoted to the meeting in general and priority issues in particular, and the environment surrounding the meeting.

But when you think of control, don't think of the ironfisted chair attempting only to get his own way. Think of protecting the meeting from the inherent negative forces that can lead to failure. Think of protecting the integrity of the meeting so that it can achieve its purpose, your purpose. Controlling a meeting in the wrong way can stifle the individual contributions and collective intelligence that make the meeting valuable in the first place. All of us have known the domineering leader or member who must always have his way. But overcontrol will not be a problem when control is focused on the *process* rather than the *contributions of the participants*. It is by controlling the process that we can best control the inherent undermining forces.

Don't be offended by the concept of control. Control is not a dirty word. Controlling a basketball doesn't mean that you don't pass to another teammate. Controlling a basketball is the only thing that will put you in a position to pass to a teammate. Controlling a meeting does not mean controlling directly what people say or even necessarily how the issue will be decided (although it can if you want it to). It may simply mean controlling some people so that everyone can have a say in order to achieve the best decision. It may mean removing from consideration nonpriority issues that create discord. It may mean tackling only the discordant issue because it is such a priority. It may mean limiting all persons to five minutes in order to cover all matters. But to the extent that you are responsible for any meeting, you have to get control of the process.

GET CONTROL EARLY

Whether it's a staff meeting or a no-holds-barred negotiation, control of the process must begin from the first moment a meeting is being considered, for you are at that very moment choosing the means to achieve a given purpose. By the time the meeting has commenced, it's too late. Too many decisions have already been made, often unconsciously, that may lead to your loss, someone else's victory, or a failed meeting. Likewise, controlling the process must continue long after the meeting has formally ended, for a meeting is almost never the goal in and of itself.

CHILDREN OF LIGHT AND CHILDREN OF DARKNESS

The American religious and political philosopher Reinhold Niebuhr argued that "children of light" (persons who seek to do good) must be armed with some of the weapons used by "children of darkness" (per-

78

sons who seek to do harm). This advice applies as well to meetings. There are many people who are fearful of the word "control." But you must learn to accept the fact that a certain kind of control is itself necessary. And you must accept the fact that anyone might use the meeting for good or for ill, for personal gain at the expense of someone else or for the good of the whole. Ideally, your goal at any meeting is to achieve results that will benefit you and your career, your cause and your company. But because others at the meeting may be in search of different goals, competition and conflict are inevitable. Don't be naive. You will achieve your goals only to the extent that you are willing and able to use the strategies that will exert a positive control over every meeting you attend.

CHAPTER SIX
Learn to Say No

LESS IS MORE.

—Mies van der Rohe

"I would venture that half the scheduled meetings in the average American company could be done away with and never be missed," IMG President Mark McCormack says, and he's absolutely right.

The first step in controlling a meeting is to *avoid* those meetings likely to go nowhere. Then it's a matter of knowing what *you* want in the meetings you do attend. Too often we automatically say yes to requests for meetings and to our own comforting inclination to hold them. Given the cumulative impact of a failed meeting, the opportunity to say no, or to say no to parts of the meeting, or to postpone the meeting until necessary preparations have been made or proper participants have been selected, is the most important choice in controlling any meeting. Don't give it away!

THE "BUSIEST MAN" AND WHY LESS IS MORE

Look to the top of your organization. Usually, there sits the person who attends the greatest number of meetings. Yet it is true that "It is the busiest man who has time to spare." In fact, at the top of any organization, one has to be able to *manage* more and more meetings —to avoid or delegate attendance as well as to run them. The busiest man actually says no to more meetings than he says yes to. The busiest man always has time to spare when he requires it, because he makes that time. His ability to say no is more important than his power to say yes in getting him to the top of the organization.

Thus, while it is the person at the top of an organization who is given the responsibility for handling more and more meetings, the corollary is definitely not true; simply having more meetings will not get you to the top. Nonetheless, this corollary has been taken for fact, causing the ambitious and nonambitious alike to seek more meetings in the mistaken belief that it will get them to the top of the organization. The truth is that it is not the quantity of meetings that will get you to the top, it's the perceived *quality* of those meetings, *who* attends them, and *what* you are able to accomplish. That is why the "busiest man" rejects more meetings than he accepts, or he alters the timing, composition, and tasks of the meetings he does attend to fit his goals. Ironically, the busiest person can handle more because he consciously makes choices to handle less.

We have seen that the leverage involved in any meeting is huge and is as likely to be negative as positive. The impact of a poor meeting (often unseen) is never neutral, and the meeting always robs time that could be devoted elsewhere. While it is said in baseball that you can't get a hit if you don't get to the plate, there are many substitutes for a meeting that can get the job done with far less risk. Five hits out of ten at bats is not a bad average in baseball. But five good meetings and five bad ones probably mean you're getting nowhere in the overall scheme of things. Further, three good meetings out of three are likely to be better than five good meetings out of ten. Obviously you are better off working for a few successful meetings than a lot of mediocre ones.

Likewise, your conscious decision to limit issues in the meetings you do attend, to focus, is a necessary substitute for the unconscious, unprioritized limitations that must otherwise occur. If you ask a student to remember ten facts, he will invariably forget three of them, perhaps the most important three. Better to focus on those three. Utilizing meetings carefully and sparingly will be more effective in achieving ultimate personal and organizational goals than will a shotgun approach that inflicts unintended damage even while you may sometimes hit your target.

"[Internal organizational] meetings are by definition a concession to deficient organization," says management expert Peter Drucker. "For one either meets or one works. One cannot do both at the same time." Such meetings are usually a sign that assignments and responsibilities are not clear. Meetings become substitutes. More mediocre meetings imply less capable management. Fewer but better meetings imply more effective management.

Whether it's a staff meeting or a meeting to pitch a deal, the first question you should ask is "Do I really need another meeting?" When you approach this question, remember you are always making a trade-off. It's not a matter of another meeting versus nothing. It's a matter of weighing the positive and negative leverage of that meeting against an alternative leverage of your time and the time of your meeting partners. It's a win or a loss.

NO-WIN MEETINGS

It often takes a good number of worthless meetings to teach you to say no. How often have you agreed to a lunch meeting only to find that the matter could have been handled by phone or letter? Unfortunately, your response to a request for a meeting is an automatic "yes" without stopping to think about what the meeting is intended to accomplish and if it could be accomplished in a less time-consuming way.

Politicians learn to say no very early in their careers. Former U.S. Senator and Foreign Relations Committee Member John Tunney points to certain types of meetings in which you just should not participate. "Obviously, both statesmen and politicians have to think about this a great deal, since you need to maintain relations and still make choices," Tunney says, "but there are certain types of meetings which are no-win situations if you go. It may relate to something on the agenda or to one of the participants or something about the timing. You simply should not be there. The statesman/politician must first ask, 'Should I attend this meeting? What will be the significance of my attendance or nonattendance? Do I win or lose simply by being there?' You cannot and should not attend a great number of meetings that others would like you to attend. Only the most amateur person or someone with vast time on his hands would do so."

Assume that you are the United States undersecretary of state and that the finance minister of a poor, developing country has asked for a meeting on a variety of issues. But, in fact, your sources tell you that she will publicly request a restructuring of her country's debt to the United States and probably has a particular plan to present. Your own government would have no response as yet to such a request, and given the volatile political situation in this underdeveloped nation, your own government has not reached a decision about the extent to which it is willing to go to support that country's current leadership. In truth, your government doesn't have a position and does not want to take one as yet. Do you schedule the meeting?

As Tunney says, "Unless the president or the secretary of state orders you to attend, you'd be a fool to say yes to such a meeting. By saying yes, you have agreed to the agenda. From there it's a no-win situation. In diplomatic language, you've implied your willingness to entertain the request merely by attending. If you say no to the request, it will be a double insult. And you can't say yes. Don't agree to the meeting in the first place."

HOLDING AN UNNECESSARY MEETING CAN
UNDERMINE YOUR REPUTATION

Of course, you don't have to be undersecretary of state to face such a situation. In many everyday situations the meeting simply should not take place.

Some time ago I was presented with a dilemma. I was then serving as the president of the board of governors of the California Community Colleges. The board consists of fifteen members appointed by the governor of California and is charged with leadership and coordination of the state's 106 community colleges, institutions with a combined budget of about $1.5 billion. I had appointed one of the board members—we'll call her Ms. Smith—to chair an ad hoc committee with jurisdiction over an area in which she claimed particular interest and expertise. Ms. Smith had already had two meetings of the ad hoc committee when she anxiously approached me at a board of governors meeting and said, "I need to have another meeting of my committee. There are some questions and decisions which have to be made that I didn't cover before."

I asked Ms. Smith if she had first attempted to resolve these issues in her own mind and if she was prepared to make particular recommendations as to what should be done. If so, there might be little need to waste the time of others with an unnecessary meeting.

"Oh, no," she said, "that's why I want the meeting. To resolve these issues."

I was frustrated. You don't chair a committee simply to sit at the head of the table. I had appointed Ms. Smith, at her request, because she claimed that she had the expertise, believed she knew what should be done, and wanted the job. I had assumed that she would review the questions and issues first to determine what recommendations she could or could not make to her committee, which issues would require study, and which were controversial and might require extended committee discussion. But she had done nothing but call meetings. And now she wanted a third! I was losing my patience and also forming a judgment about Ms. Smith.

"How do you know if you really need a meeting?" I asked. "How do you know what to focus on? How do you know if there really are 'issues' unless you've sorted them through first in your own mind or talked to the others by phone?"

To my amazement, she replied, "I can decide all of that at the meeting."

Well, maybe she could. But she was willing to call people together from all over the state to ad-lib a meeting. Wrong! As the chair of this committee she had an obligation to go much further along in the decision process before calling together her committee members for yet another meeting. It is possible that no further meeting would be required, only a memo outlining a recommended course of action and requesting any comments or objections. In that event, the matters could be settled without using the valuable time of others. She could avoid risking error, and she would have established her reputation as an efficient and effective chair.

There is, of course, another fallout from such ill-conceived, unnecessary meetings. Once you establish a pattern of poor meetings, after a while the best people don't come. The process feeds on itself, and you build a reputation you don't want. You get poor attendees and poorer meetings.

Therefore, as someone with the power to call a meeting, you must determine whether that meeting is truly necessary. As someone who is invited to a meeting, it is also *your* responsibility to decide for yourself whether the meeting is necessary and whether you have sufficient reason to attend. As someone directed to attend a meeting, it is your obligation to do all you possibly can to ensure that the meeting works for your organization, your cause, or your boss and for you personally.

MEETING FOR THE WRONG REASONS

In making the determination to attend a meeting, be aware that there are numerous "hidden" reasons why people desire to meet. Some are related to human needs. Some are related to a specific personal agenda. In determining whether a meeting is necessary, learn to ask yourself whether the following hidden motivations are really what's behind the suggestion to meet.

MEETING AS A SUBSTITUTE FOR WORK

Meetings appear to many participants to offer a rest from "real" work, or at least a break from other kinds of work. People tend to avoid their own work by calling or attending meetings. Some virtually convert their jobs into a series of meetings. Look out for those who use meetings to avoid work.

MISERY AND JOY LOVE COMPANY

When the prospect of a difficult situation arises, we all feel more comfortable if there is someone with whom to share the pain, whether or not another person's participation aids in dealing with the situation. Likewise, good news is twice as good when we can share it. Don't reject all meetings that seek to share joy or misery, but recognize them for what they are and judge their utility accordingly.

THE DESIRE TO SHARE RESPONSIBILITY AND RISK

Because decisions are difficult, it's easier to share the responsibility for making them. Holding a meeting for that purpose can be helpful, too, if you're looking for input. But sometimes it's merely an effort to avoid making a tough decision. Look out for the tendency to avoid decisions or responsibilities by holding a meeting.

PEOPLE WHO HAVE INFORMATION FEEL THE NEED TO SHARE IT

Whether it's relevant to a present task or not, people want to tell you things. Just as true, we are often afraid we'll miss something someone else might say. Meetings can be valuable networking channels; they are just as often simply gossip arenas.

THE DESIRE TO BE LIKED AND RESPECTED

Particularly when new on the job, an employee re-
lishes the time he or she can spend with peers or those
higher in the organization. They seek meetings in
order to find reassurance or attention. Meetings whose
purpose is to establish or maintain relations are useful, but they should be seen for what they are. Sometimes recognition to employees can be given in better
ways. Look out for the tendency to simply "hang out"
together in a meeting supposedly called for another
purpose.

THE NEED TO REFLECT POWER

Meetings are, necessarily, a sign of power. Appropriately or not, the person who is busy in meetings is
perceived to be on the way up. "Every company has its
quota of executives," notes Mark McCormack, "who
judge the value of what they have to say by the
number of people who are forced to listen to them. For
these executives an important meeting is one in which
there aren't enough chairs to go around." It is difficult
to avoid such meetings with those who have control
over your future. But be aware when you yourself succumb to the need for mere ego reinforcement, and
avoid meetings with peers who simply seek to gain
power by holding a meeting.

THE TENDENCY TO BE INCLUSIVE

We tend to want to include as many people as possible, whether or not they are truly necessary to the suc-

cess of the meeting. Wide participation can be healthy, but in many cases it will simply cause the creation of a smaller group that must meet to serve the function of the original meeting. The result is simply another series of meetings.

For instance, a particular state Democratic party executive committee, made up of the officers and committee chairs, existed for the purpose of setting policy and organizing the state convention. The emergence of various interest groups representing elements within the party soon forced the chairman to appoint more committees so that each of the groups—ethnics, women, gays, southern-state members, northern-state members—could have a share of the power. The executive committee was then expanded to include these new committee chairs but now reached a size too large to develop policy effectively and plan the annual convention. A steering committee, composed of the original members of the executive committee, was then formed to advise the new executive committee. Actual participation in the development of policy and planning for the annual convention by the new committee chairs did not increase, although the number of meetings required did.

WE GET LAZY

Particularly with respect to distributing information, some people just get lazy. Instead of taking the time to prepare written materials short enough to be read and detailed enough to be meaningful, they call a meeting and ad-lib. This is as dangerous as it is wasteful, since oral communication is almost always subject to more misunderstanding than written communication is.

THE CONVERTED MEETING

Be careful with meetings called for one purpose in which a member is likely to attempt to convert the meeting to another use. For instance, a meeting may be structured to address marketing, but it is really a forum to attack another employee. Look out for meetings in which you don't have notice of what is on the agenda. Neither you nor the rest of the group may be prepared.

RUSHING TO FAILURE

Look out for the presumption that any action is better than no action and therefore any meeting is better than no meeting. Just any meeting can be far worse than no meeting. Exercise some patience.

THE WAY IT IS

The most common reason we attend meetings, particularly routine meetings, is that the meeting is simply taking place, and, like a robot, we just go. These are the easiest meetings to curtail once you recognize the problem.

TRY SAYING NO

An awareness of the ulterior motives for meetings will help you decide which meetings are "musts" and which are misses. Consider saying no to every request for a meeting or any inclination on your part to call a meeting. Force yourself to justify the meeting, evaluating the need in the context of your time, your goals, and the risks of failure. You will do everyone concerned a great service.

I received a call not long ago from a client my law firm was taking public with a multimillion-dollar offer of stock. The company is well run and very profitable and was then nearly 100 percent owned by its founder and chairman. At the time of the call, our office had prepared what we believed was a near final, if not final, draft-offering circular, and the accountants (one of the so-called Big Eight) had prepared what they believed to be a final draft of the financials. The underwriter, Prudential-Bache, had set a tentative price for the stock. All of this had occurred within the previous twenty-four hours. Someone (sometime it's difficult to find out just whose idea the meeting is!) scheduled an "all-hands" meeting (including all of the parties, in this case about eighteen people) in Indianapolis to approve documents and discuss any problems. It meant that the very next day my law partner and I would have to fly to Indianapolis from Los Angeles; Prudential-Bache and its lawyers would have to fly in from Chicago; and others would have to come from the outskirts of Indianapolis.

I don't mind such traveling. And for the people from Chicago, it was less than an hour by air. But no one was *prepared* for the meeting. While it would imply some sense of momentum, it was destined for failure. Everyone would have felt as if he were working: time would be *spent*, and it would be time associated with the public offering. But the various parties concerned had not even received the respective drafts, over one hundred pages of single-spaced, tiny print. If the drafts were acceptable, why take everyone's full day for a meeting? We could get the document printed and circulate it. But far worse was the risk of the damage done in a poorly-prepared-for meeting; who could tell what the problems were and whether my client was prepared to deal with them? But because each person presumed that someone else had to know more than he did ("It's not *my* meeting"), no one objected to the meeting until I said, "Wait a minute, this is crazy. No one's prepared. We'll only lose precious time in getting this filed with the Securities and Exchange Commission. Let's review the materials separately, talk by phone, and see if we even need a meeting." Not an earth-shattering request, but because the "deal makers" were so intent on moving forward, everyone close to the deal makers had been afraid to make it. They abdicated responsibility.

Fortunately, my client was a man who listens. He delayed the meeting. As it turned out, the only thing that needed discussion was a very serious issue that, had it been brought up before all parties, would have seriously embarrassed the company. It was handled quietly and effectively with the minimum number of people necessary involved. In hard dollars—perhaps the least costly expense—the parties saved tens of thousands of dollars by deciding not to meet. In exercising some patience, my client avoided the risk of blowing the deal.

SAYING NO TO ROUTINE MEETINGS

You should be no less ruthless in cutting out "routine" meetings or regularly scheduled staff or committee meetings. "Routine meetings often become groups looking for subjects," notes former Shaklee Board Chairman Gary Shansby. The question is, "Is this a meeting with a patterned agenda or format that absolutely requires routine scheduling?" If the answer is no, take it off the schedule.

As a general rule, it is not good enough to say that a routine meeting is simply an opportunity to get together and see what's up. One friend of mine has said, "If there's nothing up, I just cancel it." But these required cancelations are losses! Nothing is more debilitating than supposedly "routine" meetings that are regularly canceled and have no real purpose. Regularly canceling or rescheduling routine meetings disrupts the calendar of those who have arranged their own work plans to fit the meeting. It is a disorganized leader who requires others to shift their own calendars on his whim. He has lost sight of the impact of his enormous leverage. Furthermore, an often canceled routine meeting begins to lose its importance and urgency. Attendees prepare less fully, knowing that the meeting may be canceled or rescheduled. And the meeting itself will degenerate. Others will follow your pattern and regularly cancel their regular meetings, creating more losses.

It can be a tough decision to remove these meetings from the "routine" category. There is often implicit some kind of policy change and the fear of the negative impact upon regular attendees. But you aren't doing anyone a favor by keeping these meetings on the calendar only to be canceled. Instead, borrow a concept from the political world. The decision to do away with a meeting is a "one-day story." To continue the meeting is to perpetuate a continuing failure. So, from time to time, try to practice "zero-based scheduling of meetings." That is, review all of your routine meetings to see if they are still worth the "routine" label. And when you add a routine meeting, ask which other routine meeting you are willing to eliminate.

A WORD ABOUT ROUTINE MEETINGS AND POWER

Nothing reflects power like routine meetings. They give direction (even if it's wrong), require regular attendance, and maintain a pecking order. If power is your goal, try to develop excuses for routine meetings. You will begin to control a portion of the work week of all attendees. But if effectiveness is your goal, try to eliminate all but the absolutely necessary routine meetings. If you are trying to deny others power, try to prevent them from holding routine meetings.

THE "NO AGENDA" MEETING

There's a difference between a "routine" meeting and what some people regularly schedule as a "no agenda" meeting with a key aide. Such a meeting provides them an opportunity simply to let go, to dream about the business. They catch up on each other's work, they socialize. When kept to one or two people who share common interests and responsibilities, such a meeting can be very useful. But be careful. If a "no agenda" meeting has no specific purpose, it can easily be a waste of time. Ask yourself what you want and what you've gotten out of these meetings before you continue scheduling them.

HOW TO MAKE THE CHOICE

How do you decide to hold or attend a particular meeting? First, recognize that more often than not you do, indeed, have a decision to make, whether you are calling a meeting or attending one. You will not offend people by saying no to all or part of the meeting if it is necessary to do so. Saying no is the best way to avoid a poor meeting and force the structuring of a better one.

Second, even in the most obvious situations or circumstances over which you seem to have little control, look for the following critical signs of when *not* to hold a meeting, or at least when to say no to parts of the meeting, its composition, or its timing:

1. You can't say what you want to accomplish or what the meeting is supposed to accomplish.

2. Notwithstanding the purpose, you don't believe the meeting will serve it by virtue of its authority, composition, or timing.

3. The intended purpose of the meeting is better accomplished through another tool or process.

4. Attending this meeting will preclude holding another, more effective meeting.

5. You cannot be prepared.

6. The leader of the meeting will not be properly prepared. He doesn't know how to run a meeting, and nothing can help.

7. You cannot control the meeting to achieve your ends, and your absence will require rescheduling.

8. The meeting will have the wrong mix of people or won't have the right people.

9. The meeting environment is wrong.

10. The meeting is not the best use of your time.

HOW TO SAY NO

How do you learn to say no to meetings? Here are some suggestions:

Ask the leader what his objective is. This forces the person who wants to hold the meeting to be specific about the goal, and he may reevaluate the best way to achieve it. It's something you should do as a participant anyway. Where appropriate, ask about other elements of the proposed meeting: Are these the right people? Is this the right time? Do we have all the facts?

State the deficiency. If he knows and trusts the person well, University of California President David Gardner notes the missing element of a proposed meeting, as long as doing so does not result in an insult or create further confusion. Stating the real deficiency in a proposed meeting is a good habit to develop with fellow workers, since it educates others with respect to good meetings and establishes a pattern for well-structured meetings. If done properly, it is a habit that will fairly quickly permeate the entire organization.

You can do the same thing during the meeting when particular issues are not appropriate. For instance, if you're at the marketing meeting and someone wants to act on staff salaries, note that the necessary preparation has not occurred or that the right people aren't there or that it will take time from the stated purpose. Defer action. Likewise, if you're attending a board meeting and a brand-new action item is proposed, seek to assign it to an appropriate committee for presentation through the normal process. Recognize that simply because you are meeting doesn't mean everything that can be discussed should be discussed at that time.

Ask if your attendance is necessary. If your boss is meeting constantly and, you believe, unnecessarily with the entire staff, you might simply ask whether he'd rather have you attend the meeting or finish some other project. This will take some confidence on your part that you don't *have* to be at every meeting, good or bad. Approach your boss as a member of his team. It won't insult him when he understands your motives are in his best interests.

Claim a scheduling conflict. Sometimes you'll find you're not the only one who thought it was a bad idea to meet. The meeting may never be rescheduled.

See if a telephone call works instead. "John, can I just give you my input by phone?" Sometimes it's all that's needed to deflect the overmeeter.

Just say you're "not available." In many instances you need say no more. By the time you get back to rescheduling, the perceived "need" has often passed.

Have someone else respond for you. Your secretary can take the heat.

Change the nature of the meeting. One of the most sophisticated examples of avoiding a meeting I've ever seen occurred at my own expense. It's an example of how to say yes to one part of a meeting and no to another. A board member and I were very concerned with the behavior of our organization's chief executive officer vis-à-vis board members. We asked for a meeting with the CEO for breakfast one morning but foolishly confused the matter by adding another item for discussion: the finances of the organization. (I had ignored the rule that meetings fail in direct proportion to the number and kinds of issues addressed.) As a result, the CEO brought along to the breakfast his staff member best prepared to answer budget and finance questions. As a matter of courtesy and protocol, discussion of personal board relations was not appropriate until after the staff member left the room. But the CEO used all the available time to discuss the finance questions, and we were forced to adjourn the meeting without getting to the primary subject on our minds. In essence, the CEO attended the one meeting (on the budget) and avoided the other (on the matter of board relations). I had called the meeting, but I lost control. A few days later the CEO called to set up a meeting on the issue of board relations. By that time he had done some radical homework and was able to diminish the severity of the problem. You can't do that very often without offending board members. But, in truth, we were never sure if it was all intentional or not. If so, we agreed, it was a brilliant move. Perhaps, we thought, the time had not been correct for us to have called the meeting in the first place!

YOU HAVE A CHOICE!

Most of the time you don't have to be either sophisticated or Machiavellian in saying no to a meeting. You simply have to recognize that you have a choice whether or not to attend or whether at least to influence its composition, timing, and structure. Once the meeting is "on," you're at a disadvantage in correcting

100

flaws. Whether dealing with routine meetings or with ad hoc meetings, learn to ask yourself whether the meeting is really necessary. By doing so you'll naturally cut down on wasteful meetings and force improvements in the ones you eventually do call or attend.

Learn to say *no*!

Part Three

STRATEGIES FOR HEADING YOUR MEETINGS IN THE RIGHT DIRECTION

Methods of locomotion have improved greatly in recent years, but places to go remain about the same.

—DON HEROLD

CHAPTER SEVEN

Start with the Right Attitude

MAN OFTEN BECOMES WHAT HE BELIEVES HIM-
SELF TO BE. IF I KEEP ON SAYING TO MYSELF THAT
I CANNOT DO A CERTAIN THING, IT IS POSSIBLE
THAT I MAY END BY REALLY BECOMING INCAPA-
BLE OF DOING IT. ON THE CONTRARY, IF I SHALL
HAVE THE BELIEF THAT I CAN DO IT, I SHALL
SURELY ACQUIRE THE CAPACITY TO DO IT EVEN IF I
MAY NOT HAVE IT AT THE BEGINNING.

—Mahatma Gandhi

RECOGNIZING the general tendency of meetings to fail
may encourage you to be cynical about many would-
be meetings, but you should never be cynical toward
the people with whom you do meet. Just the opposite.
While you've got to be aware of the natural pitfalls in
meetings in order to prepare for them and use them to
your own advantage, the attitude you take toward your
actual partners should be positive and supportive.
Be more selective about your meeting partners, but
give more to those with whom you do meet.

In thinking about any meeting, you should begin
with the hypothesis that you're going to attend only
meetings that matter with persons whose attendance is

necessary to effect the purpose of the meeting. It will be worth your time being there, you can accomplish your goals, and your meeting partners are critical to the outcome. That being the case, you *need* your meeting partners, and you almost always need to *show it.* Whether you're negotiating a deal with an "opponent," delegating an assignment to an employee, or brainstorming with your staff, your meeting partners are the real essence of the meeting. The meeting is not the table and chairs, or the room, or the paper generated. The meeting is that engagement that occurs between and among human beings.

REFLECT AND MAINTAIN HIGH EXPECTATIONS FOR YOUR MEETING PARTNERS

In both politics and sports, much is made of the phenomenon of "momentum." Anyone who plays tennis or golf—or any sport—knows the feeling he gets when he's "in the groove." Psychologists may explain it as nothing more than confidence. Moves become sure and strong, while the opponent "loses momentum," becoming unsure and weak, unable to "get it going." Whatever it is, we perform better when we believe in ourselves, our "teammates," and the opportunities for success.

It has been shown that high expectations by schoolteachers may alone be enough to cause an increase of twenty-five points in their students' IQ scores. In another study, adults were given ten puzzles to solve. The participants were told their scores at the end, but the scores were fictitious. Half the group was told it had done well, the other half was told it had scored poorly, though in reality the scores in both groups were mixed. All were then given another ten puzzles. The group that was told it had done well (and in fact they had all scored differently) all did better on the second series of puzzles. The group that was told it had scored poorly in the first round (and many had done well) all fared more poorly on the second series of puzzles.

Meetings that require group productivity are no different. If the group believes that what it does cannot make a difference, it won't put out a confident effort. But if the group believes in itself, productivity will increase. Therefore, if you want the best from your meeting partners, set high expectations for the success of your meetings and the success of your meeting partners. Make them believe that (1) the group is worth being with; (2) individual members will have an opportunity to influence the outcome; and (3) the cause is one that warrants their attention and effort.

A meeting in which expectations are too low, or one in which the feeling is that individual contributions are not necessary or that the task is not important or meaningful, is a meeting doomed to mediocrity. Such a meeting also sets expectations for any future meetings called by the same leaders or even with the same participants, since a pattern of failure or mediocrity has been established.

Of course, if you want your meeting partner to perform poorly, make him feel small, remind him of previous mistakes, make him think he is less than capable. Maintain the appearance of courtesy so that he doesn't blame you. Make him think it's his problem, his weakness, his deficiency that will cause him to fail. But if you really want contributions, treat your meeting partners with respect. Some of them are going to be smarter than others. Some will be more creative. Some will be better workers. Some will be more influential. Don't shortchange any of them. The meeting is under way, and the decision has been made that they're all important or they wouldn't be there. They are now all part of your team; if you want positive results, your challenge is to allow each one to contribute the best that he or she is capable of contributing.

HIGH EXPECTATIONS OF EFFORT

Equally important is the effort you expect from the individuals attending the meeting. A recent study found that the more rigorous and demanding the requirements for membership in a meeting, the more the participants will enjoy the meeting and its members and the more they will contribute. The members seek to contribute effort at the level of expectations held for them, and they seek to maintain those expectations. By contrast, the same study found that where the meetings did not occupy the same level of importance, where it was not viewed as serious business, the meeting deteriorated.

You should not feel timid, therefore, about demanding serious preparation, attention, and effort from meeting partners. The more common problem is not that you ask too much, but that you ask too little of each other. Set or imply high standards for membership and participation and you'll be more likely to achieve better results. People want to belong to a club that has tough standards.

REASONABLE, ACHIEVABLE EXPECTATIONS

There is a profound difference between setting high expectations for success and effort on the one hand and setting unrealistic goals on the other. Goals that are not achievable will, in fact, establish expectations for failure.

Everyone likes to think of himself as a winner. Make your partners feel like winners by setting up winnable situations. Studies have shown that most companies set goals too high, ensuring some degree of failure. Excellent companies set goals that can be met, reinforcing a positive sense of self. Excellent meeting leaders set objectives that can be met and challenge the meeting partners to meet them.

I AND THOU

You will get more from your meeting partners if you speak in terms of "we" instead of "I." The group is ultimately credited with a team win or a team loss. You'll discourage contributions and increase jealousies if you talk about "my idea" or "my plan." Instead of saying "I think we should raise prices," try "What if

109

we raised prices?" Instead of "My idea is to refer this to committee," try "How about referring this to committee?"

When the group has made progress, talk "we." When you're proposing goals, talk "we." When you're claiming success, talk "we." And when you're tempted to take credit, talk "we."

SPECIFIC SUGGESTIONS REGARDING EXPECTATIONS

In suggesting a meeting: As the leader, make the task appear important and cause the participants to believe in the value of their participation. As the participant, once you decide to attend, speak positively about the goal and the other meeting partners.

In the beginning: "As the meeting opens," says Metropolitan Theatres owner and CEO Bruce Corwin, "it is important to communicate a sense of confidence to those present. People are quick to sense absence of confidence or nervousness, and this can spoil not only their enjoyment of the meeting, but also their faith in the leader and their willingness to contribute. They will sense the negativity and contribute negativity, almost subconsciously." As a participant, don't begin by being negative about your presence, the purpose, or the facilities. Even if you intend to be critical of a plan or idea, make your first comments positive.

Throughout: Unless you are purposely trying to undermine someone or some idea, try to look for what's

110

positive in any statement made. If you must disagree, disagree with what is said—not with who says it. As progress is made—for instance, as you move from one stage to another—note it. Congratulate the group as you move on. Create the impression that the team has a hitting streak going.

At the end: I serve on a special commission with a member who always seems to have to say something negative at the end of a meeting, even when he thinks it's been a good meeting. He may refer to a matter discussed and concluded much earlier, or he may raise a "concern" he has over something considered at a previous meeting. He is very sincere and, when he's on topic, contributes a great deal. Recently, the chair turned to me and said, "Why does he always make these negative comments at the end of the meeting? No one's listening to the substance, really. All they hear is the negativity. It makes more work for me."

Unfortunately, last statements are often the ones the group remembers. The last comments and discussion will establish a sense for the success or failure of the meeting and expectations about the next one. By the end of the meeting, members have begun to "turn off" substantive discussion. The last few moments of a meeting should be reserved for summarizing actions and creating expectations for future meetings. Try to end the meeting with the sense that expectations were met, even when much was left to be desired. Simply focus harder on the next meeting.

In general: Always bring a positive attitude to any meeting. Don't knock your partners or the assignment unless you're seeking to undermine the meeting. You'll only make any task that much more difficult. Be particularly careful not to bring other problems you may be having into the meeting. It's surprising how many people begin a meeting by telling you what a bad day it's been. You will only program yourself and the meeting for failure. Program yourself and the group to win, and you will increase your chance of winning.

CHAPTER EIGHT

The Cardinal Rule:
Never Attend a Meeting Without Knowing What You Want to Accomplish

---

THE MAN WHO SUCCEEDS ABOVE HIS FELLOWS IS THE ONE WHO, EARLY IN LIFE, CLEARLY DISCERNS HIS OBJECT, AND TOWARDS THAT OBJECT HABIT-UALLY DIRECTS HIS POWERS. EVEN GENIUS ITSELF IS BUT FINE OBSERVATION STRENGTHENED BY FIX-ITY OF PURPOSE. EVERY MAN WHO OBSERVES VI-GILANTLY AND RESOLVES STEADFASTLY GROWS UNCONSCIOUSLY INTO GENIUS.

—Edward G. Bulwer-Lytton

NEVER attend a meeting without knowing exactly what you want to accomplish and how you intend to ac-complish it. I'm not talking here about knowing what you want only in some major deal or negotiation. Nor am I talking about having only a vague notion of your goals. In one-on-one negotiations, for meetings with staff, for sales meetings, for planning meetings, and for business entertainment meetings, if you don't know

113

precisely what you're looking for, you're headed for a failed meeting. So before walking into any meeting, you must ask yourself what you want to have accomplished when you're walking out.

WE MAKE TIME TO MEET BUT TAKE LITTLE TIME TO THINK ABOUT MEETING

Most of us tend to schedule meetings feeling that somehow "it will work itself out." We casually attend staff meetings without an agenda or with an agenda so ill-defined as to be meaningless: mere discussion topics with a goal nowhere in sight. We make appointments for "business lunches" without a purpose, only with the thought that it's "good for business." We go to other meetings in a state of trance, particularly when we make the additional mistake of thinking they "belong" to someone else. We assume we have a goal, although we seldom take the time to articulate it. We quickly make the time for the meeting but seldom take time to think about what we want to achieve. That's a prescription for failure. If you don't have the time to think about what you want, you shouldn't make time for the meeting.

Think about a typical day in your own life and list the various meetings you attend. How often do you really ask yourself before meeting what it is you will have accomplished when the meeting is over? Not a general perception of "what it's about," but a clear understanding of what you hope to achieve, what kind of decision will be made, what problem will be solved, what action will be taken, what information can be learned, what feeling will be conveyed, what value will have been created? In the majority of meetings, insufficient attention is given to articulating the exact goal. We tend just to go.

DON'T PRESUME YOU OR OTHERS KNOW WHAT THE GOAL IS

Unless you know what you want to accomplish, you're wasting your time and that of your meeting partners. You're leveraging failure. Don't presume that what you want to accomplish is understood, even by you. You're just dreaming. Too many meetings are called and run on the assumption that everyone knows what goal is being sought. As we have seen, everyone naturally develops a different notion of what the meeting is for. So many forces can undermine the meeting that when you and the group don't know what you want, it's virtually hopeless. Force yourself and others to define the goal of every meeting. You'll be surprised how a few minutes of thought about your goal will change your whole approach in meeting with a disappointed employee, a high-performing salesperson, a tough competitor, or a potential partner.

EVEN THE BEST FAIL

I was having lunch one day with the chairman of the board and chief executive officer of a prominent national investment company, a bright, talented, experienced, and unusually creative man. Before lunch he had given me a tour of his offices and facilities. He was proud of his early and major commitment to state-of-the-art equipment of various kinds and the resulting increased productivity that put him ahead of his competitors. He was equally proud of the progressive incentive program he had developed in consultation with his employees. I was extremely impressed with the extensive goal setting, planning, analysis, evaluation, and follow-up that seemed to characterize his management style and run throughout the company. In short, here was a top-notch CEO who knew what he wanted and how to get it. The company's earnings only confirmed it.

I was therefore rather shocked at the conversation we had during and after lunch. I was certainly not surprised—and only too happy to help—when he asked me to set up a meeting with Chuck Manatt, the then-chairman of the Democratic National Committee. From our lunch conversation, it was clear my CEO friend was interested in government and economics, and I knew that Chuck Manatt would be most interested in meeting any businessman who might be a potential contributor to the Democratic party. It seemed to me a good fit. Then, just as I was leaving, the CEO asked me if I could give him any advice with respect to this proposed meeting with the national party chair.

"Well," I asked, "what's your goal for the meeting? What do you want to accomplish?"

He looked at me blankly. "I'm not sure. I guess I want to change the economic policy of the Democratic party. I thought we'd talk basic theory at first." Becom-

116

ing a little nervous, he went on to say that maybe he did not have his whole economic plan quite ready just yet.

I laughed and noted that changing the party's economic policy, to the extent that any political party has one, would probably take more than one meeting.

"Perhaps," he said, "I'm not ready for a meeting."

"Perhaps," I responded politely, "you're ready for a different meeting from the one you thought you wanted."

But in truth I was surprised. Here was the successful CEO of a major company asking for a meeting with the national chair of one of the country's two main political parties, and he didn't have a goal or an understanding of the use of this meeting in achieving it! Nor did he appear to be the least bit aware that Chuck Manatt, a real "player," would have his own goal and agenda for such a meeting. In a matter of minutes, Chuck would have made the meeting his own.

In fact, the CEO was *not* ready for the meeting he thought he wanted. He hadn't given it enough thought. He had not focused on what his ultimate goal was and what purpose this meeting could serve in achieving it. After some discussion, we decided more clearly what he wanted (a relationship) and what role a first meeting with Chuck might play in achieving it. Ultimately, this extra thought before scheduling the meeting helped make it effective rather than inconclusive or possibly even embarrassing, for it forced him to focus on Chuck Manatt rather than economic theory.

By assessing what you want before you schedule any meeting, you can more effectively plan to bring it

117

about. You can also anticipate countermoves. And you can avoid rather harsh judgments about your basic abilities, either as a leader or as a member of the team.

WHAT TASK ARE YOU ASKING THE GROUP TO ACCOMPLISH?

In attempting to accomplish a group goal, meeting partners actually attempt to complete a particular "task." More than a single task can be (and usually is) sought in most meetings, but the tasks are still distinct. There is a tendency to mix these different tasks together, however, without recognizing that the individual or group with whom you're meeting may not understand what specific task is being undertaken at a particular time. Thus, the task may be to *offer advice,* but the group thinks the task is to *make a decision.* You may want the group to *give factual information,* but the group thinks the task is to provide *subjective advice.* Some tasks are inappropriate for some groups. Some tasks are incompatible with a particular meeting, although the participants will quite naturally attempt them. In planning a meeting, make clear what task it is you're asking your meeting partners to perform. In attending a meeting, make sure you know what's being asked of you.

Here are the basic tasks and most common problems associated with them. After articulating what it is you want to have accomplished when the meeting is over, clarify your goal by learning to describe it in terms of the tasks required of the group. And remember, the more you limit the number of tasks in any single meeting, the more successful you are likely to be.

1. *To give or exchange information.* We meet to give, receive, or share information. Such information can be transmitted in a variety of ways at a meeting. The most common would be an oral report or a written report supplemented by an oral report.

As a general rule, meetings are overused to transmit information. They are better used to *clarify* information already provided. Information can be provided in ways that are far more efficient than oral or written presentations at meetings. Among other things, our ability to comprehend written information is three to four times greater than our ability to comprehend oral information. Using a meeting to give information should set off an alarm bell: Could any of the material be presented in writing before the meeting? If so, either somebody's not being efficient, or someone's trying to put something over on you. When you're looking to reduce your meetings or to reduce the number of tasks, look first to cut down on those that seek only to inform.

While information can be gathered efficiently in small meetings lower in the structure of an organization, information gathering is flawed at high-level meetings. That is, information can be shared, but it should be gathered elsewhere; otherwise it is almost always incomplete. At high-level meetings you are better served by delegating the task of information gathering.

2. *To create or develop ideas.* We meet to generate ideas. Except for the most complicated and esoteric brainstorming (as, for example, the kind done over time through exchanges in academic journals), meetings are the best way of brainstorming. Properly structured, brainstorming meetings provide the opportunity for rapid, creative stimulation

that is difficult to achieve through other means.

Perhaps the greatest problem with brainstorming meetings is that we try to conduct them like any other meeting. Brainstorming requires great openness and freedom, the license to make mistakes. Meetings to accomplish other tasks usually have a more authoritarian structure. It is difficult to create the proper environment for brainstorming, but it is more difficult still to move from one of the other tasks to brainstorming or from brainstorming to one of the other tasks. You simply have difficulty letting go. As a general rule, brainstorming meetings should be conducted for that purpose alone. At least make sure that all ideas are on the table before you begin critiquing any of them.

3. *To decide on goals or issues.* A meeting is a good forum for decision making when a decision requires the assent of more than one person and when you want to enhance commitment to a decision. But be careful to distinguish between assent and consultation. The act of *deciding* must also be distinguished from steps that *lead* to the decision, including information gathering and issue clarification, brainstorming and persuading. Meetings called "to make a decision" are sometimes really meetings required to gather information for a decision to be made elsewhere. Or they are called to make a decision that is not ripe for the making; the steps preliminary to the decision have not occurred. The board of directors of a company can't gather the information at the board meeting. It must be done by staff, or it will be incomplete. The greatest problem with decision-making meetings is in understanding what part of the decision-making process the group is in.

A second major problem is that the group is merely going through the motions, rubber-stamping a decision that has already been made. When someone says that the purpose of the meeting is to make a decision, ask yourself whether all of the steps preliminary to making a decision have been completed. When you ask others to meet to make a decision, ask whether everyone has had access to the information generated in preliminary steps. Otherwise your participants won't be ready, and your meeting to decide will become something else.

4. *To delegate work or authority.* We meet to assign tasks and to delegate work or authority. A function of management and communication, such a meeting allows for clarification and amplification of an assignment not always possible in a memorandum or phone call. It can also allow the group *as a whole* to delegate assignments among the participants and therefore to commit to the assignments together. But sometimes a meeting to delegate is an excuse for the leader not having been able to define what is sought. The group may be incapable of delegating fairly and productively among participants. More often still, delegation is the forgotten task. At the end of any meeting, ask the questions "What now?" and "Who needs to do what?"

5. *To share work or responsibility.* Meetings provide a forum in which work can be done jointly—for instance, the codrafting of a letter or analysis of facts. But these tasks are difficult for groups of any size to perform. Most of them involve a series of other tasks. Meetings called to share work are often schemes for avoiding work, reinforcing management expert Peter Drucker's admonition that we either work or we meet, we can't do both. They also may reflect work done poorly elsewhere. Large meeting groups often flounder attempting to do work that has been done poorly or incompletely by staff or committees. The work by the large group will also be flawed, and time will be taken from tasks that are appropriate. With board meetings in particular, you will be better served if you refer the work to others. In so doing, you establish standards for others.

121

6. *To persuade, involve, or co-opt.* Meetings are often called with the express intent of persuading someone of something. Also, merely including someone in a meeting can serve to involve or co-opt them. Since changing someone's point of view is not easy, proper preparation is all the more important. So is the environment. Meetings to persuade or co-opt sometimes try to do too much at one time. Make sure that anything that *can* be done before the meeting *is* done so that meeting time can be focused on your goal.

7. *To inspire.* We meet as a matter of ceremony or ritual in order to inspire respect, trust, faith, dedication, or some other value. The validity and power of this task are underrated. Such meetings may be accompanied by another specific task, but ceremony may be so important as nearly to override the other purposes. One such example would be the inauguration of a president. Another might be a groundbreaking ceremony for a new building.

In many meetings, the need for inspiration or the fact that it is the principal task sought is not understood by planners, let alone attendees. Therefore, elements that should be directed toward inspiring (grand location, majestic music, or eloquent rhetoric) are overwhelmed by elements intended to serve other purposes (usually providing information). Be careful that you do not bring into these meetings goals and tasks that are inconsistent with the basic task. Also, as a meeting leader, remember that every meeting must inspire the group to commit to the task.

8. *To establish or maintain relations.* There may be no other purpose in a particular meeting than maintaining or establishing a relationship with someone you intend to meet with again. The surest way to undermine such a meeting is to forget your purpose and become involved in conflicting interests. For example, debating politics and

religion may be stimulating, but it may not be particularly productive in business and professional meetings whose purpose is to establish common grounds for positive relations.

9. *To socialize and have fun.* For both business and nonbusiness meetings, the common problem here is to again forget the purpose and be drawn into other tasks that will encourage anything but fun. Since business and professional groups have business and profession in common, business is the first thing meeting partners tend to discuss. But it's often the last thing you should discuss, particularly when spouses are present. The judgments made at social engagements involve your social skills. The participant who can't carry on a nonbusiness conversation is seen as limited. Before attending social events involving business associates, give a little thought to the protocol of the event and nonbusiness topics of discussion. Be interested in your fellow participants and their personal lives.

10. *To consult.* We meet to receive advice and counsel or to give advice and counsel to others. The three most common problems here are (a) defining the problem; (b) setting the environment for good consultation; and (c) confusing consultation with making a decision. Everyone has a limited view of any problem. Defining the advice you seek is critical. Also, if you really want input, you'd better say so. Your behavior may suggest exactly the opposite. Finally, make clear who's going to ultimately make the decision.

WHAT KIND OF MEETING IS THIS?

Because the way you handle a meeting depends upon the purpose or tasks you seek to achieve, it is important to learn to identify before you attend which basic task or tasks you hope to undertake. When a meeting bogs down, there's a good chance that the participants have lost sight of the task. When meetings fail, it is often because the parties were confused as to the basic task from the start. Were they supposed to get information? To make a decision? To draft a proposal? To maintain relations? All of these things? If so, in what order? Many meetings, if not most, serve more than one of the aforementioned tasks. A committee might be expected to receive a report, identify problems, and make a decision in a single meeting. There is nothing wrong with this as long as the group is clear on what task is being served at any given moment and it is the right group for *each* task. Some of the tasks sought may be inappropriate, while others may be perfectly correct. You cannot float willy-nilly from one to the other. The group will have enough trouble when it is focused on a single task; when the task keeps changing, group competence diminishes.

David Corvo, executive producer of *CBS This Morning*, says, "I'm stunned by the number of people who don't know what kind of meeting they're in. One of the best examples is when the boss convenes a meeting to convey a decision that has already been reached, and a staff member persists in debating the decision. The time for that is past! You're in the wrong meeting. *This* meeting is informational and delegatory. By continuing to question the decision, you are only showing your own poor judgment and insensibility to the boss's purpose and needs."

It is equally important to recognize what kind of

124

group is meeting and where the group is in the process of carrying out some series of tasks. In general, groups composed of subordinates cannot effectively develop policy because they lack the authority or perspective. In general, groups of superiors cannot gather information in the meeting. Too many boards attempt to find information or draft resolutions *at* the meeting. Too many task forces skimp on the facts. Ask yourself, "What should be done by this group, and what should be left to someone else?"

Of course, knowing what you want to accomplish does not mean you should be closed to opportunities that may present themselves. If a surprise opportunity offers itself, grab it.

LIMITING WHAT YOU WANT TO ACCOMPLISH

Since the risks of failure are as great as the chances of success, you ensure success by limiting what you want to accomplish. Initially, that means limiting the tasks in a particular meeting. Then you must make sure that everyone who will attend clearly understands the nature of those tasks and is capable of achieving them. The meeting that tries to accomplish too much is as dangerous as the meeting without a clear notion of what it is supposed to accomplish and what task is required.

The simplest way to bring a focus to each of your meetings is to set a goal. Everything else follows from where you want to go. So before any meeting, ask yourself, "When this meeting is over, what is it that I want to be able to say I've accomplished?" Be specific —and make sure that everyone else who will attend the meeting is aware of that goal.

CHAPTER NINE
Distinguishing Success from Failure

LET US RAISE A STANDARD TO WHICH THE WISE
AND HONEST CAN REPAIR.

—George Washington

IF someone asks you, "How'd the meeting go?" and all
you can say is that it was a "good discussion," you're
in trouble. Every meeting is a win or a loss. The only
way you'll know if you've won is if you develop some
yardstick by which to judge your meeting. A meeting
to inform is not a successful meeting unless a prede-
fined amount of information has been presented *and*
received. A brainstorming meeting is not successful
unless a certain number of ideas has been generated. A
meeting called to delegate is not successful unless
each participant has left with a clear understanding of
his respective assignment. You will have had a successful negotiation only if you can distinguish in advance those points you must win from those that
would be nice to win and those unnecessary to win.

For any meeting you attend, therefore, you must set
a measurable objective prior to the meeting by which

127

you can distinguish success from failure when the meeting is over. Only then can you say whether a meeting was a "good" meeting. For instance, if you were to decide to hold a meeting in order to provide information on a new billing system to be used in your office, ask what your specific goal is with respect to the results of the meeting. How much of the information can you reasonably expect your meeting partners to remember? Will you be pleased if they remember 50 percent of what was presented at the meeting? Will you be disappointed if they don't remember all of what was presented? Or should you expect that *going into* the meeting, they will already know 75 percent, and that the meeting will be used to reinforce the more difficult remaining 25 percent? Which specific items do you believe *must* be understood for the office to function? How will you know what has been heard and remembered as opposed to what has been said?

To cite another example, if you've scheduled a meeting with your boss about a raise, what is it this one meeting can achieve? What will make it a successful meeting? Does he really have to give you a raise today to make it a success? Will you feel it's been successful if he says he'll consider it? If it's your routine staff meeting, what do you want each participant to be thinking as he leaves the room? What you say is less important than what they hear.

Be as specific as you can about a measurable objective against which you can judge the success of your meeting. You want to be able to answer the question "Was that meeting a success—and if so, why?" The simple exercise of targeting the specific goal will change your approach to the meeting dramatically, for it will force you to recognize the limitations of the meeting as well as to assess your objective prior to, during, and after the meeting. In fact, it may convince you that the meeting is not your best available tool for accomplishing your objective.

IS YOUR STANDARD REASONABLE?

Meetings should have *attainable* standards. Is it reasonable to distribute a ten-page memorandum at the meeting and expect valuable comments? Will you judge the memo sound if no one responds? Is it reasonable to expect your boss to give you a raise today? Or is it more reasonable to expect him to say he'll consider it if you will get back to him with information on salaries for comparable jobs? Perhaps, then, would it make sense to know the information on comparable salaries before you talk with him? Setting reasonable standards to judge the meeting requires some thought and may even alter your perception of what you hope to achieve.

I used to sit on a public education board in California that was having trouble getting what we considered to be a fair budget from the then new governor of the state, George Deukmejian. In order to provide an opportunity for the governor to signify a commitment to our educational system, we offered him the opportunity to appear before us at one of our official board meetings. Fearful of being publicly embarrassed at such a meeting, the governor obliged in part but also countermoved. He would be happy to meet with us but wanted the meeting on his own turf, in his office. He did not want a public meeting. We needed the meeting more than he did, and in any case, he was the governor. So a meeting with our full board—a meeting very different from the one we originally intended—was set in his office and limited to thirty minutes.

We had to determine what we wanted to accomplish in this environment and in this limited time frame. Our strategic goal was adequate funding for the community colleges. But, clearly, in thirty minutes we would not have time to get into great questions of policy or numbers; and everyone would have different specific policies and numbers. Furthermore, some initial reconnaissance told us that this relatively new governor, in particular, dealt primarily through staff on policy and fiscal questions; we would do better to talk to his staff in a separate meeting about policy or details. Finally, since each of us had been appointed by his predecessor, former Governor Jerry Brown, we knew George Deukmejian had suspicions about us concerning everything from our politics to our commitment and competence.

What should our purpose and objective be? And what standards could we use to determine our success?

We were not about to change the governor's politics, and he was not about to change ours. Therefore, as president of the board I suggested that the best we could do in thirty minutes was to begin to convince him of our commitment and our competence, that we could work together. My specific objective was to have the governor conclude following the meeting, "They are not such a bad lot. They seem to know what they're doing and what is needed, and they care. They are bound to generate credibility with others." At least, after that, he would have a harder time dismissing us and the colleges. We could then be in a position to have a follow-up meeting with his staff or with him at another time, and in such a follow-up meeting we would discuss substantive matters on an entirely different basis—communication would be more open. The objective of this meeting, therefore, would be limited. The standard for success would be the extent to which each of the board members could demonstrate courtesy, commitment, and competence.

Of course, we had board members who strongly disagreed with this approach. Some of them didn't believe a meeting with the governor of another political party could be valuable at all, and therefore any strategy was worthless. We could "wing it," depending on how the governor acted. (It did not occur to these board members that the governor would be making a *judgment* about us, based on how we handled the meeting, that would affect future budgets.) Others wanted to argue about the governor's previous budget cuts. "Let's give him hell," one said. But how could we gain from that? Others wanted to tell him that he didn't understand the real issues. Presumably they personally were going to begin to educate him. Fortunately, these board members went along with the decision of a majority who were convinced that such approaches would lead nowhere. When forced, no one could say what they wanted to accomplish by such a potentially acrimonious meeting.

Thus, everything we did in preparing for that meeting was directed toward our objective: to create with the governor and his staff the impression that we were competent and that we cared. We began by delivering well in advance a detailed memorandum regarding the board's basic agenda for the coming year. If the governor read it, so much the better. More important, we knew delivery alone would reflect that we were on top of things and had a vision of where the organization should be headed. I asked two friends who knew members of the governor's staff to make phone calls prior to the meeting commenting positively on the ability of particular board members. To begin the meeting, I made a formal but courteous and positive introduction of the board to the governor. Each of us was prepared to say something that would serve to introduce ourselves and our areas of concern and competence. One of our members demonstrated particular knowledge of the budgetary process by expressing concern about a noneducation item close to the governor's heart that was blocked in committee. Another noted a mutual friendship with someone from the governor's hometown. We arrived on time, demonstrated an understanding of protocol, and encouraged the most articulate of us to speak most often. In short, we simply looked good and competent. We carefully avoided anything that would detract from our objective. Because the decision to proceed in this way had been made jointly by board members, each felt compelled to do his or her part regardless of personal feelings.

Some might argue, as one activist friend of mine said, that there was no substance to this meeting; that we were "afraid" to tackle difficult questions; that "debate" is healthy. But we were clear in our minds about the goal for *this* meeting and what would distinguish success from failure. There would be other opportunities to be substantive or tough. Board members bit their respective tongues to meet the objective, and in terms of our standard, it was a successful meeting.

And it worked. The very next day the governor's education aide called to say how surprised and impressed the governor was with the board. He related that they had discussed the meeting in a staff session that morning, and the governor wanted more information about our agenda and plans. The governor's chief of staff would follow up with our chancellor immediately.

The result we achieved was due to our ability to determine in advance what we could realistically accomplish and to set a standard by which each person could assess his own performance. Subsequent efforts would have to carry the ball farther. We might not get farther. But we were now moving up field, still in the game.

WHEN YOU'RE NOT SPECIFIC ABOUT WHAT YOU WANT

Not all meetings work out as well as our meeting with the governor. A few years ago, for example, I arranged through a mutual friend to have a drink with Jerry Foster, vice president of Pacific Telesis, then called Pacific Telephone, to promote a nonprofit organization on whose board of directors I was then serving. Foster is Mr. Pac Tel in southern California, with strong influence in the business community. I suppose that in the long term I was looking for some kind of financial support from Pac Tel or at least increased credibility from the downtown Los Angeles business establishment for the organization. I viewed the meeting as an opportunity to establish relations with Jerry Foster for this organization, but in truth I really had not set a specific objective for the meeting or a standard by which to distinguish success from failure.

Now, the fact that someone with Foster's stature and influence was willing to sit down and discuss a nonprofit organization was a statement of sorts. At this point in his career, he assumed that he and Pac Tel would be asked for something. So while agreeing to such a meeting was a courtesy, it also meant that the door was open. At an initial meeting like this he would want to know more about the organization, its purpose, and its ability to execute its purpose. So I gave Jerry a terrific pitch about the organization. He was clearly impressed. He thought that the cause was more than worthy and seemed moved by my energy and commitment. I could feel the momentum building until finally he said, "Well, George, what can I do to help you?"

I stammered a bit and replied, "Well, I guess you could just talk up our efforts among the business leaders you know, and I'll be getting back to you sometime soon."

Suddenly, Jerry Foster's smile drooped and he asked the waiter for the check. I had wasted his time. Clearly, I didn't have an objective for the meeting. He didn't want another meeting—which seemed to be what I was asking for with my response. He had been led by our mutual friend to believe I was the kind of person who knew what I was doing. He had been prepared to help. But obviously I had not thought out in advance what it was I wanted from him. By my response to his question, I seemed to demonstrate that I wasn't such an organized and directed fellow after all. If I didn't know what I wanted from Jerry Foster in one simple meeting, how could I make a success out of this organization—for making it a success would require success in hundreds of meetings just like this one. Just as important, I had delivered a message that I was not necessarily someone he would need to know in the future. He had given me a slow, fat pitch down the middle of the plate, and I'd let it go by for a strike!

I should have been prepared with a definitive request for assistance: a contribution to the organization, a letter to the other executives, use of his name in a fund-raising letter. Going in, I should have realized that I had no basis upon which to distinguish success from failure. Therefore our meeting was unlikely to be a success. It took me a full year to get over my chagrin and schedule another meeting with Jerry Foster. Fortunately he agreed, and that time I knew what I wanted to get out of our meeting. Specifically.

MAINTAINING YOUR OBJECTIVE AND MAKING YOUR MOVE

Had I known what I wanted from Pac Tel, of course, I would have had to *ask* for it. And that raises a major

point about setting objectives and standards to measure success—having the fortitude, the chutzpah, to
maintain your objective.

In many meetings there is at least one major move
that must be taken by you to accomplish your objective. For a salesman or deal maker, it is often referred
to as "closing." It is where the timid shrink and the
winners step forward. "The Move" can be a formal
motion at a board meeting, a request for business or
assistance, the firing or praising of an employee, or the
first kiss on the first date. Clearly, making your Move
is important.

The Move is not always obvious, and in certain
types of meetings, particularly regular staff meetings
or brainstorming sessions, most of the Moves should
be left to the chair or leader. But you'll always have
your own objectives as well. As a general rule, the
more specific the objective, the more specific the
Move. In any event, if you get your lip to the cup,
you've got to be willing to drink. In other words, you
must always be willing to make the move that will
permit you to achieve your objective.

It was not long after my meeting with Jerry Foster
that a young friend of mine—in fact, the son of my
former personal physician—called to ask for a meeting. He had recently completed his Ph.D. work in political science at Harvard. He came to my office, and
we spent about twenty-five minutes talking about
everything from the Celtics to his family. Having set
my own objective, near the end of the meeting I asked
him if he could provide me with some research that
related to this book. He was honored to oblige, he said.

We began to talk about this section of the book, making the Move. As we finished discussing the importance of making the Move, he exclaimed, "My God, that relates to why I wanted to talk to you. I wanted you to help me get an article published in the *Center Magazine!*" (a journal on whose board of directors I served). It seems that asking me to help him get an article published was his basic objective for the meeting, but he had never gotten to it. Had we not discussed this chapter, he would have left without even asking me to help. He had done everything but make the Move. I asked him why.

"Well, you seem so busy with so many things that I didn't want to impose," he said.

"Forgive me," I countered, "but if that is what you are worried about, you've already imposed. You've taken my time and yours. Worse yet, you did not accomplish what you set out to do. It's as if you put on your bathing suit, drove to the beach, but couldn't get out of your car."

"I know," he responded. "I guess I chickened out because I thought you might say no. And I was afraid of making a bad impression."

"Let me help make it easier for you to ask in the future," I said. "Try to remember that there are people out there who are better at meetings than you are. They expect you to have an objective for a meeting, and they expect you to make the move necessary to achieve it. If you get to the water's edge and can't get wet, you've made a far worse impression than if you made your move and were turned down in your request. You can't be afraid of a 'no.' It's part of asking."

137

SHARE THE SPECIFIC OBJECTIVE AND THE RESPONSIBILITY FOR ACHIEVING IT

Once you have set measurable objectives by which to distinguish success from failure, *share* them with the group. When someone who participates in a meeting can see the specific, tangible objectives of the meeting, he or she can focus on getting there. You know how important specific goals are for you personally. They're just as important for the group. Don't hide the ball, share it.

For example, if the purpose of your meeting is brainstorming, focus the challenge sufficiently for participants so that the ideas that emerge are clearly related to the problem you are trying to solve. Otherwise you'll get ideas, but they won't relate to what you're trying to accomplish. Then, go further and set a goal of coming up with a *specific number* of ideas, usually far more than you think you need: "We're working for ten ideas. No criticizing any of them until they're all on the table." Sharing the specific objectives puts responsibility on your meeting partners for the success of the meeting.

Share the objective before the meeting if at all possible. A manager I once worked with delighted in surprising all of us as to the purpose of his meetings, let alone the standards for measuring success. His meetings went nowhere. If you want an employee to come to your office for a meeting, if possible let him know in advance what it is you want out of the meeting.

138

Permit him to contribute. Let him visualize the goal line. Then, when he gets to your office, restate the objective before you begin asking questions. If he knows what you want in advance, he can be prepared to help achieve it.

DON'T FORGET THE MEETINGS WITHIN MEETINGS

In certain meetings, sometimes called "musters," the exchanges with your individual meeting partners may be of more value to you than the basic purpose for which the group was called together. These minimeetings should have goals and standards to measure success as well.

The most obvious example of a muster might be the happy hour at the end of the week in some companies or the nearly obligatory cocktail party preceding a dinner meeting or convention. Sometimes it is understood that a group of people will simply meet at a given time with no particular business or agenda in mind. That does not mean there is no purpose to these meetings; the purpose may be to socialize or maintain relations. But even in unstructured social situations with your business associates, your performance and contributions are being measured by other members of the group, just as you are measuring theirs.

The first point that should be emphasized regarding this type of meeting is the extent of freedom given the individual participant in meeting whatever *his* or *her* purposes may be. In this "laissez-faire" or "free market" atmosphere, such meetings presume that the pursuit of an individual's interest will result in achieving

139

the meeting's purpose. Thus, the fact that a real estate deal is discussed by two members attending a cocktail party of the Boy Scout board seems not only perfectly acceptable but desirable since it maintains relations, may be fun, and inspires a continuing interest in the board.

When you're planning a muster meeting, such as a cocktail gathering, the key is to create the environment and incentives so that individual participants are naturally encouraged to act in a way that benefits your purpose. A muster meeting is difficult to rescue once it's begun, because there is little opportunity for intervention. You must create the environment, put the people in place, and from there on, it's very much out of your control. As an individual, however, you have tremendous freedom to establish your own objectives and conduct minimeetings with the participants. Unfortunately, these occasions often look like those junior high dances where the boys and girls remain with their own small group of friends. No one asks anyone to dance, and no one meets new people. You ought to look at the muster differently. The generalized purpose of a muster leaves you free to seize opportunity. Ask yourself what you want to accomplish. Set a measurable objective. Then go for it.

Perhaps your objective is as simple as meeting new business contacts at a conference. If so, set an objective that you'll establish contact with five new persons. Then get the job done. And remember, in this situation follow-up is at least as important as making the original contact.

Alan Rothenberg, one of my law partners, recognizes that part of his role as a senior partner at the firm's social events is to "dispense grace," and that associates and young partners look to him for attention and approval. If you're in such a position (and almost everyone is, relative to someone else), set your objectives accordingly. Recognize that everything you say or do will be "leveraged" by your position. Rothenberg arrives early at these events. While he enjoys them to some extent, he treats them as a part of his job: he makes a list before he goes into the meeting of the people with whom he believes it would be beneficial to visit. Sometimes his stated purpose is to follow up on a litigation case, but that's often just his way of getting a conversation going. Most of the time, he wants to give attention to someone with whom he hasn't had much recent interaction, to maintain relations. He sets an objective for each encounter and does not leave the meeting until he has met his quota of objectives. Success is measured by whether he met the quota and whether he has left each person with a positive feeling about himself and a positive feeling about Rothenberg and the firm.

SPECIFIC STANDARDS FOR MEASURING SUCCESS

How do you know if your own meetings are heading in the right direction? Try these exercises:

1. Recall a recent, typical meeting in your organization. Ask yourself: Was there a goal for the meeting?

Did you have a goal? Did you have a specific objective and a plan to achieve that objective? Was each participant aware of the objective and his part in achieving it? How successful was the meeting? Would you describe it as a win or a loss? In the end, was it really necessary? If you had to do it over again, what should be done differently?

2. Try doing a short memo summarizing briefly the actions of a particular meeting that you've already agreed to hold or attend *before* you hold or attend it. In other words, do the minutes of the meeting before it takes place. Do these minutes by first establishing in your mind your goals and objectives. Define the actions taken in terms of your definition of success. After the meeting takes place, compare your minutes with what actually happened.

3. As you're walking down the hall to a spur-of-the-moment meeting, simply ask yourself three questions:
   a. "What kind of task is sought in this meeting?"
   b. "What do I want to have accomplished when I walk out of this meeting?"
   c. "What will distinguish success from failure?"

   When you leave the meeting, ask yourself whether you were correct about the task and whether you met your objective, whether other participants were clear about the task or the objectives, and whether the meeting was a success or a failure.

4. For any meeting you are going to lead, ask the three questions outlined above, then share that information with your meeting partners before the meeting and see if it helps you achieve your goals.

Distinguishing Success from Failure

In order to know whether any meeting is successful, there must be some standard going in by which you can measure the meeting going out. Distinguish success from failure before the meeting and encourage your meeting partners to do the same.

Part Four

STRATEGIES FOR ACHIEVING YOUR GOALS AT EVERY MEETING YOU ATTEND

Go to the ant, thou sluggard; consider her ways, and be wise: which having no guide, overseer, or ruler, provideth her meat in summer, and gathered her food in the Harvest.

—PROVERBS 6:6–8

CHAPTER TEN

Prepare More and Meet Less

IN ORDER TO SPEAK SHORT UPON ANY SUBJECT, THINK LONG.

—Hugh Henry Brackenridge

ONCE a meeting has begun, variables to achieving success have already been sharply reduced. Even once you've established what distinguishes success from failure, 75 percent of success still depends upon further preparation. If you can spend more of your time in preparation, you will spend less than an equivalent amount of time in meeting, and you will be far more likely to achieve your objectives.

So, as a general rule, prepare more and meet less. Most people spend too little time in preparation and too much time in meeting. When they get to the meeting they find their hands tied, and time is wasted doing things that should have been handled prior to the meeting, or great energy is spent averting a meeting disaster that could have been avoided with a little forethought.

Envision the Meeting in Advance

For the meeting master, preparation means more than developing a laundry list of agenda items. For the participant, preparation means much more than merely reviewing materials distributed in advance. In each case, the key to proper preparation is in *envisioning* the proposed meeting long before you ever attend. Preparation means envisioning a series of meeting scenarios in the context of the meeting's goal, your objectives, and the persons attending. That includes pursuing your vision by determining what must occur prior to the meeting to allow the task to be effectively undertaken and to make your vision the final reality. It includes envisioning likely questions and problems so that you can deal with them, if possible, in advance. By the time the meeting takes place, you will already have had the advantage of a number of mental dress rehearsals.

University of California President David Pierpont Gardner, when serving as president of the University of Utah, was asked by the White House to chair the ultimately very influential National Commission on Excellence in Education, which rekindled the debate on education. The report produced by the commission is considered by many to be the single most important cause of the national resurgence of interest in education reform. While it describes a whole series of meetings rather than a single meeting, Gardner's account of his appointment (with my own analysis in brackets

148

and emphasis added) provides a wonderful example of the role of visualization in ultimately permitting a long series of meetings to be successful:

> When I was asked to serve as chairman by Education Secretary Terrel Bell, I *looked ahead* to exactly what things *could be accomplished* and *what conditions were necessary* to allow the meetings to accomplish them. I told him I would only agree to serve under these conditions. The conditions were to be essential *if I had any reason to suppose success for the commission.*
>
> First, there would be no political test applied to the appointment of any commissioner. [Composition: Gardner wanted the best people, with the best balance and with reputations sufficient to enhance the standing of the commission. With a political test controlling participation, he envisioned a "political" commission and a noncredible report.]
>
> Second, the secretary would give us a charge and then leave us alone. [Authority: He needed authority in order to attract the best people and be credible himself. If the secretary could intervene at any time, Gardner's control of the process would be challenged by others.]
>
> Third, we would be allowed to appoint our own staff. [Quality and Control: You're only as good as the staff—they prepare the work for each meeting. They had to be loyal to Gardner. Otherwise he foresaw a battle with the staff and divided loyalties.]
>
> Fourth, I wanted enough money so that we would not have to come back and ask for more. [Tools and Impressions: He envisioned what might occur if the commission ran out of money and had to go hat in

149

hand for additional funds. It might require a quid-pro-quo. Coming back for money also implies mismanagement and failure. He foresaw the risk of being second-guessed.]

Fifth, I wanted a commitment to publish our report. [Authority and Quality: Knowing the report will be published makes everyone accountable and creates authority. Gardner envisioned the problems of a commission with poor attendance.]

Sixth, we had to agree on the time line. [Authority: Timing would make or break the report. He had to be able to release the report when and only when the commission was ready.]

Seventh, the White House, the secretary of education, and I would have to agree on every appointment; in other words, neither the secretary nor the White House could force anyone on the commission. [Sharing Responsibility: This would mean the White House would "own" the report but would not force acceptance of members without Gardner's concurrence.]

I believed that these things were crucial in structuring the commission so that it would later be effective. I said I would accept only under those conditions.

Gardner adds a postscript:

A few days later I got a call from Terrel Bell saying that the White House wanted to know my political affiliation. To me, this was a sign that all of my conditions might be picked apart one by one. I said, "If you're going to ask that from me, you're going to ask it of the others, and I can't serve under those conditions." After further assurances, I accepted. They didn't bother us again. All this occurred before I decided to say yes or hold a single meeting. Of course had I waited until I said yes or until the first meeting, it would have been too late. We would have spent all our time arguing over these issues, or we would simply have been ineffective. I'm convinced to this day that the mental preparation I went through ultimately permitted a successful commission.

QUESTIONS TO HELP YOU PREPARE

Decide what you want to accomplish in a meeting. Then, in order to assist you in envisioning the meeting, ask yourself the following questions:

Do I have the authority to get the job done? If you're the boss, the answer to this question may be immediately clear. But particularly in a meeting with peers, you must be certain before you begin that you have the authority to lead the meeting and to represent the group in its decision or recommendations. You must have a mandate, usually from someone of higher authority, and your peers should be aware of it. If you are attending a meeting, you also want to be sure that the group itself has a mandate to undertake the task. Otherwise your work could be irrelevant.

Who? Who's attending the meeting, or who should attend? Whose attendance will make it more difficult to conduct a productive meeting? Whom must you speak with before the meeting? Who will be supporting you and your positions? Who will be opposing you and your positions? Too many meetings are overly inclusive or overly exclusive. Ask why you're including or excluding anyone. "Every time you add or subtract someone, you change the entire chemistry of the meeting," says Arista President Clive Davis. What steps can you take prior to the meeting to ensure the right "who"? Finally, who will not be at the meeting but will have a stake in the outcome or will place pressure on those who attend?

What? What are the priority issues that must be discussed and/or decided? In what order? Given what you desire to accomplish, have all necessary preceding steps been completed? Do you have enough information? What additional information will you require? What additional information are others likely to require? What is your personal judgment about the issues? What is the opposing point of view, and what merit does it have? Is compromise good, acceptable, and in what way? What must be done before the meeting to ensure effective use of the meeting in undertaking the task?

Where? Where should the meeting take place? How is your control or the group's creativity best served by location? How is the purpose of the meeting best served? Who suffers from what location? Is there any protocol affecting location?

When? When is the appropriate time for the meeting? Does it depend on other events? Do other matters and events depend upon this meeting? And what is the appropriate length of time for the meeting—fifteen minutes, half an hour, an hour?

How? What will be the *process* for the meeting, and how will decisions be reached? Consensus or majority rule? Consultation and benevolent dictatorship? Is there already an implied understanding with respect to this process? Who will object to the process? Are there customs and rules or etiquette that must be followed? Who should be consulted about the process and the agenda?

There are literally hundreds of different ways to prepare for the myriad meetings we have every day. The only way you will know what is required in a particular case is to envision the proposed meeting *as you would like it to take place.* As you picture the meeting you will naturally note questions and deficiencies. This visualization technique is useful whether you're attending an interview, a staff meeting, a negotiating session, or a business lunch. Preparation consists of mentally reviewing each step of the meeting in advance and then taking steps to lead the meeting in the direction you want it to go.

DO YOUR HOMEWORK

There is almost no excuse for not doing the necessary homework required for a meeting. Yet people don't do it. Not only does this slow the meeting terribly, but it sends a message to all attendees that the person who fails to do homework for this meeting probably fails to do his homework in general. It is a sign of disrespect for yourself and for others. It is very clear to meeting masters who does their homework and who does not. But if you haven't done your homework, don't broadcast it by asking questions and making comments that give you away unless you have already established a solid reputation.

GETTING OTHERS TO DO THEIR HOMEWORK

Almost as bad as not doing your homework is discouraging others from doing theirs. Let us assume that a bundle of materials for a meeting has been distributed well in advance on a rather routine item. Then, at the meeting, the leader proceeds to walk the group through the materials page by page. Not only does this take up valuable time, it sends a message to every member that preparation is unnecessary. It removes responsibility from others. Whenever you can, you want to encourage responsibility from others.

Because there are enough things that can go wrong during the meeting no matter how well you prepare, don't add poor preparation to the list. Do your homework and establish incentives for others to do theirs.

GOING BEYOND EXPECTATIONS

The most successful executives, political leaders, and educators are looking for people who stand out from the pack. The safest way to do this is to go the extra mile in preparation. It's safe because you do not have to try to dominate the meeting or risk confrontation to establish your special identity. No one will fault you for outpreparing everyone else. And it won't hurt the meeting, either.

Indiana attorney Greg Hahn told me about his former partner, John J. Dillon. "Even if he had little time, he'd always try to do at least one more thing than was expected. Expectation was the key for him. I remember when he was to be brought in for this important case regarding the rights-of-way for railroads. He used every hour he had to prepare for the get-acquainted meeting among the various lawyers and principals. He looked up all of the terminology he possibly could regarding railroads and railroad rights-of-way. I remember him saying, 'This is only a get-acquainted session. But they're going to be assessing me just the same. I want them to get acquainted with someone they *think* knows a hell of a lot about railroad rights-of-way.' He really didn't say all that much at the meeting. He didn't have to. But he made his points, and he was asked to take the lead. He simply went beyond the expectation of what was required."

Ask yourself before any meeting what it is you might do to exceed the general expectations regarding preparation. Guess the expectations, then exceed them. You might simply place one extra phone call to get an expert's opinion; you might bring to the attention of other members an article or magazine piece; you might carefully review the minutes to find a single error that you can correct; you might find a particular

set of statistics you think would be helpful. Remember, you're not trying to embarrass anyone else—
and your contribution must be relevant. But a few
minutes of additional preparation will give you credibility with your meeting partners not only on the
issues for which you've specially prepared but for
other matters as well.

Doing your homework indicates what kind of person you are. Getting others to do their homework indicates what kind of leader you are. Going the extra
mile, exceeding common expectations, sets you apart
from the group.

COUNTING VOTES

"If I have something on the agenda that is really important to me, I always know where the votes are before I go into that meeting," says lawyer and
investment banker Peter Kelly. By doing this, you can
make a judgment to move ahead on your item, to do a
little extra homework, or to take it off the agenda if
your count shows you can't win.

I don't know why so many people tie their hands by
limiting their persuasion to what occurs *during* the
meeting. It's not illegal or improper; it's often necessary. By the time you get to the meeting, positions may
have hardened. People are flattered to be approached
individually. It affords you the chance to hear things
you will not hear at the meeting. So always consider
whether you need to talk with participants before the
meeting. And always presume that the sophisticated

participants are talking to other members before the meeting.

THE INNER GAME OF MEETINGS

The process of preparation is something like the process suggested by Timothy Gallwey in his popular book, *The Inner Game of Tennis*. He advises picturing each shot in your mind before and as you hit it. You'll substantially reduce the number of mishits, he says. Preparing for a meeting is much the same. Thankfully, you've got more time. There are myriad rules for conducting an effective meeting. But among them all, preparation is nine-tenths of the law. Visualize the meeting in advance. Picture the perfect attitude of the group, the perfect location, the perfect proposal, the perfect discussion, the perfect argument. Visualize the perfect response to the difficult participant. Visualize the perfect meeting and then make the necessary preparations to make that vision a reality.

CHAPTER ELEVEN

See Yourself as Others See You

O WAD SOME POW'R THE GIFTIE GIE US
TO SEE OURSELS AS OTHERS SEE US!
IT WAD FRAE MONY A BLUNDER FREE US,
AND FOOLISH NOTION.
—Robert Burns
To a Louse

"REMEMBER," says Henry Rogers, chairman of the national public relations firm of Rogers & Cowan, "to the other guy, you're the *other guy*."

People tend to see what they want to see. They pick out facts that support preconceptions, including preconceptions of you. The other guy doesn't see you the way you do. How could he? He sees you only as you are to him, perhaps just a small part of your own life. He's meeting with an image of you based upon your working relationship, your reputation, the way you treat him, and the way you treat others. He doesn't *really* know you; he cannot possibly understand the entire context in which you speak. Don't expect him to.

Unless you can get some notion of the context in which others see you, miscommunication, and sometimes serious miscommunication, is inevitable. Try to put yourself in the other guy's shoes, not so you can agree, but so that you can understand him well enough to communicate. Understanding his thinking is not just useful, it's absolutely necessary. Differences between people are really differences in how they perceive. Therefore, take the time to analyze how your meeting partner perceives you. It will help you understand how he thinks and how you can reach him.

Putting yourself in the other guy's shoes is a matter of understanding his personal situation and his perception of the issues. Understanding his perception of you is primarily a matter of recognizing your standing role with him—peer, superior, subordinate—since that role will dominate any perception he has of you. Other perceptions will relate to your personality, character, habits, and power: Are you viewed as fair? Tough? Strong? Vindictive? Do you have the authority and power to do what you say?

The natural tendency in a meeting—and a prime contributor to the failure of meetings—is to act toward our meeting partners in a way that actually discourages the contribution we want from them. We tend to be too tough with subordinates, too supple with superiors, and too friendly with peers.

MEETINGS WITH SUBORDINATES

Subordinates have a difficult time seeing you as anything other than the keeper of their futures. Their basic desire, therefore, is to please. Control, the operative word, is fairly easy to maintain with subordinates because of this inherent power relationship. You have the recognized authority to establish the parameters of discussion, the issues of importance, the problems that need solutions, or the tasks that should be done. When you require control you can merely take it. Therefore, while control of the meeting *process* is always critical, your inherent power to control that process is not the basic problem in meetings with subordinates. The problem is freeing the subordinates from their natural tendency to defer to you in order to permit honesty and worthwhile engagement.

When meeting with subordinates, intimidation usually serves little purpose except to quell contribution. While you may require intimidation at selected times, in general you will be better served if you look for ways to appear less intimidating, more open.

When meeting with subordinates, you are also dealing with persons who are usually not in a position to understand the whole picture as completely as you do. Stating clearly what it is you seek from them is critical. Otherwise, they can easily misconstrue your objective and can be too broad or too narrow in their response, or they may simply attempt to please you, looking for signs of favor or displeasure. If you set clear parameters to discussion while permitting as much freedom as possible within those parameters, you'll be more likely to get valuable input. You should be just as thoughtful about what you are saying by body language and facial expressions as what you say with words.

DELEGATING

In meeting with subordinates, you spend a good deal of time delegating. Again, your authority to do so is clear. Concentrate on making your direction clear. Your subordinate is hearing many things you may not mean to be saying. Whether you think he's justified or not, he's anxious about you. He won't hear things clearly. You should be less interested in what you say than in what he hears.

From time to time try encouraging a group of subordinates to delegate among its members the particular tasks that come out of a meeting. It focuses subordinates on the task rather than on pleasing you. The members will "buy in" to the delegation process and will have a stake in the completion of each other's work. Encourage them to establish their own objectives by which success and failure are distinguished.

LOOKING FOR SOLUTIONS

When seeking input for solutions from your subordinates, look for more than one solution. You will leave yourself options, and you will encourage more participation. Once you show favor for any particular course of action, there is a tendency for subordinates to jump on that bandwagon. Reserve judgment and use your authority to liberate rather than to inhibit ideas.

MEETINGS WITH PEERS

In meetings with your peers, your right to control is not as clear as it is with subordinates. In fact, your authority can be resented and challenged. The more informal your authority as leader, the tougher your job. Yet you must have clear control of the *process* in order to lead a meeting of peers and get what you want as a participant. Thus, getting control and maintaining control in a healthy way *is* very important in meetings with peers.

That is not to say you should be unfriendly or cold. In fact, you will need friendship and humor to encourage cooperation and to dispel hostility. Simply remember that the meeting is a natural arena for competition among peers. In order to accomplish your objective, particularly as chair, you must compete for control of the process. Here are some tools that will help you obtain and maintain control in your meetings with peers.

THE BLESSING

Being blessed by a superior won't give you as much authority as that superior has, but it will go a long way. If you have been assigned by your boss to lead a group of your peers in making recommendations for cost control within the company, your job is going to be a whole lot easier if a memo goes from the boss to each group member noting that he has given you that responsibility. You have been anointed. It will be more difficult if he's said to you alone, "Bill, get these people together and see what they say about cost control."

Even if your mandate was simply an oral request, you can still control the parameters of discussion if you communicate that mandate to the members of the group: "The boss believes there is a problem with distribution in the South. He's directed me to chair this committee and to get back to him on our progress and proposed solutions."

THE AGENDA

Here, more than anywhere, is where control of a meeting of peers originates. Through a precise statement of what the meeting has been called to accomplish, you can gain a great deal of control over the process. A working agenda, among peers, usually requires some consultation or agreement on items beforehand, since peers perceive that they will have an equal voice in the meeting. Don't ignore consultation! Use the consultation process to your advantage. Your leadership role comes not from simply creating the agenda out of whole cloth, but in consulting with your peers and shaping the agenda accordingly. Members will presume that you and you alone possess the input from all other members, and their role will shift subtly in their minds to a quasi-subordinate one when you possess the whole picture. But as soon as it becomes clear that you have not consulted on the process, your control is threatened.

Consulting with your peers also gives you the opportunity to get at the "hidden agendas" and an understanding of the needs of your meeting partners. You will have more information than your meeting partners, and that information will help you in getting what you want from the group.

FORMALITY

It is more difficult among peers to gain control than to give up control. It is more difficult to move from informality to formality than from formality to informality. When in doubt, begin on a more formal basis with your peers. Always be friendly and courteous, but establish your respect and authority before becoming informal. Loosen up as your mandate is accepted and your control is clear.

SUCCESS

Nothing breeds authority like success. If you can develop a pattern of successful meetings, your peers will be more likely to give you the authority you need. Let them believe they are always dealing with success when they deal with you. Everyone wants to work with a winner. But remember, they are still your peers. Give them the credit they deserve, or you'll risk jealousies and the loss of your authority.

MEETING WITH SUPERIORS

In meetings with your superiors, you are a resource person. You are there for your expertise, knowledge, or information, and that is the way in which you are most effective. As a clear subordinate, you cannot see the whole picture, nor do you have the responsibility or authority to affect it. If you try to control the process, you'll lose. Any effort to create a mandate or control the agenda will be viewed as a threat to superior authority, and your credibility will be challenged even in areas where you should be the expert. Your role is to present facts, identify problems, and propose a solution. You certainly don't want to be a yes-man, but in meetings where you are subordinate, you don't want arguments, either. You cannot win them. In essence, with a group of superiors, you are an interloper, a foreigner.

Your strength as a subordinate comes from your expertise and from the clarity of your expression of that expertise. Your opinions are less desired than your knowledge. You should avoid expressing subjective views unless asked, but be candid and honest about what it is you perceive and understand regarding the issue in question.

While in meetings with peers it's necessary to have a mandate for leadership before the meeting begins, when leading (for instance, making a presentation) a meeting with superiors, you need a mandate for *action* once the meeting is over. Of course, you should have established prior to the meeting what you want to have achieved when the meeting is over. Usually that will be a direction to move forward or not move forward on some task. Do not leave without a mandate from every member whose approval is important to the task ahead of you. Get commitments for further meetings and for further direction. Review and fix dates if at all possible.

MEETING TOGETHER WITH PEERS, SUBORDINATES, AND SUPERIORS

It's often difficult for multiples of superiors, subordinates, and peers to work together productively in a meeting. Concerns about authority and competition are magnified. But if you find yourself heading a meeting of persons with clearly differentiated rank, some of whom report regularly to others in the meeting, and if you really want input, call on the lowest-ranking members first. That way you'll be more likely to get their honest input. Once their superiors have spoken, they will be more inhibited. The superiors, on the other hand, will be less inhibited from disagreeing with a previous statement by a subordinate.

In summary, it is important in any meeting both to see yourself as others see you and to present yourself as you want to be seen in order to obtain your objectives. When leading subordinates, give up control. As a superior you can always retake it. Be clear about what you want, but encourage contribution. When leading peers, get a mandate in one form or another and gain control of the process by controlling the agenda. But seek input from your peers for that agenda prior to the meeting and share credit for whatever the meeting accomplishes. When leading superiors, you can't really "lead," so don't try. Prepare thoroughly, present complete information about a problem as well as a possible solution, and seek a clear mandate for the future tasks you are assigned. When leading with all three, call on the lowest-ranking members first when you really want input. Call on higher-ranking persons first when you want conformity.

Finally, the member who overlooks the inherent nature of his relationships with meeting members will elicit the wrong kinds of contributions from them and will send the wrong message about his ability to lead. Before *any* meeting, ask yourself what your standing relationship is to your meeting partners and how you can use that relationship to achieve the goals you have set for the meeting and for yourself.

CHAPTER TWELVE

The Theater in Meetings

THE DRAMA'S LAWS THE DRAMA'S PATRONS GIVE.
FOR WE THAT LIVE TO PLEASE MUST PLEASE TO
LIVE.

—Samuel Johnson

THINK about your last meeting. Maybe you had drinks
with a prospective customer or client. Consciously or
unconsciously, you chose a suitable setting for this
meeting. You probably engaged in some verbal fore-
play, discussing a number of nonbusiness issues—the
World Series, politics, the weather—before getting to
the subject matter that brought you together: his business. You tried to be entertaining, interesting, and interested. In discussing your work, you probably
"painted a picture" of your company and what you
could do for him. In one environment or another you
might have pulled out charts and graphs, discussed
trends and statistics. Yet you still hadn't reached the
meat of the meeting. You were establishing yourself as
a person worth listening to, setting a frame of mind,
trying to find things in common, so that what you
were about to say would be more credible. You told
the prospective client how attentive your company

could be and supported your contention by demonstrating your enthusiasm. Finally, you made a pitch for his business. Then you finished with more polite conversation so that your meeting ended on a friendly, warm note.

In essence, most of your meeting time was not spent talking *directly* about your objective. You were "setting the stage," using various means of communication to get your points across and influence the prospective client's attitude toward you.

ALL MEETINGS ARE THEATER

All meetings require communication, and all communication is assisted by theater or theatrical techniques and devices that complement the verbal message. Theater is far more important in meetings than is generally assumed, not just because it allows communication to be more effective, but also because—intentionally or unintentionally—it can very easily undermine the objective. You communicate something with everything you do—how you sit, where you choose to meet, how you dress, the tone of voice when you speak, the energy you create in a room. You cannot "eliminate" theater in a meeting any more than you can eliminate location or costume or seating. There is always some location, some mode of dress, some seating—some theater—all of which conveys some message. You can't eliminate these secondary messages, but you can control the message by controlling the theater. And as long as there will be theater, you want it to enhance your objective.

THEATER AS ENTERTAINMENT

People listen and contribute more effectively when they are engaged. It is not just what you put on the table that is important; it is more important what your meeting partners are able to digest. But holding the attention of meeting partners is difficult. Facts alone don't taste good. Some degree of entertainment—theater—is required to maintain engagement, particularly as the meeting goes on. The theater may exist in the drama of the problem or the risk of failure; it may exist in the force of personalities. But theater as entertainment is not a luxury. It is a necessity. Theatrical techniques are required to engage your meeting partners in the substance of the meeting. Maintaining the engagement of your partners is no less your responsibility than is the success of the meeting itself. Although an interesting meeting doesn't guarantee a successful one, a boring meeting is almost never a good meeting because it means the group was less than fully engaged.

BEFORE THE MEETING

Before the meeting ask yourself how you can theatrically draw the attention of your partners to the objective you've established for the meeting. Think about opening humor; think about break points and techniques for refocusing attention. With respect to each issue, think about how you can give life to the words and facts that will bombard the participants. And think about what theater—discord, disorganization— you want to avoid. Think about your own "perfor- mance" and what image you want to project in the meeting.

CHANGE THE TEMPO

Washington political consultant and adviser Ted Van Dyk offers theatrical advice from his days as a musi- cian. "Don't play the same kind of song all the time. Play a fast song, then a slow song. Change the tempo and you are more likely to keep interest high." Try not to make the meeting one report after another or one long debate on an issue. Mix it up a bit. Provide a break so that interest can be renewed.

MAKE YOUR MEETING PARTNERS INTERESTED
BY MAKING THEM INTERESTING

I once attended a meeting of potential supporters of Senator Gary Hart when he was seeking the Demo- cratic nomination for president. The meeting was con- vened by the invitation of John Emerson, then deputy national campaign manager for Hart. Most of those in- vited were not familiar with their fellow guests. In be- ginning the meeting, Emerson went around the rather large table of twenty-five people and asked each of them to introduce himself. That's not uncommon. But Emerson went further. We had all been pretty dull in talking about ourselves. So, after each guest modestly said his name, Emerson told us all something special about that person, something intended to make us ap-

171

preciate each individual's status, power, and appeal. The result was that each person attending, upon hearing how special everyone else was (and no one was as special as Emerson made us *feel*), felt honored to be in the group and truly interested in his fellow meeting partners. When Senator Hart spoke, everything *he* said was a bit more interesting by virtue of *who* was at the table! Applying that same principle to a business meeting, you can be sure a participant will be more engaged when he believes that his meeting partners are special and he belongs in the group. If it's the same old group of people, try noting something current and positive about a particular member before he speaks, such as "John just finished a terrific report on our western clients."

SHOW YOUR OWN INTEREST

If you're not interested, why should anyone else be interested? Show your own interest in the matters under discussion at a meeting. It's infectious. Your attitude should be enthusiastic even if the task at hand is rather routine and mundane. Enthusiasm is infectious, too.

EXPRESS AND ALLOW FOR EXPRESSIONS OF HUMOR

Look for opportunities to inject humor into a meeting, if it is not at the expense of another participant. And don't be afraid to let others express humor as well. Often a particular member is simply good at injecting humor into a meeting. Don't be jealous. It will only help keep the meeting interesting.

THEATER FACILITATES THE MESSAGE

A second reason theater is important is more subtle: the theatrical techniques you utilize in a meeting can facilitate or inhibit communicating a particular message. Obviously, if you show up for an interview on Wall Street unshaven and dressed in jeans, you will have a harder time being heard by an investment banker. Your costume is wrong. If you smile while lecturing a subordinate, he will not take you seriously. The spoken word is only part of communicating. Your dress, your body language, your punctuality, your attitude—all are sending messages as well. This kind of "theater" is almost never neutral. It always says *something*.

THEATER AS THE MESSAGE

The third reason theater is important is something of an extension of the second: theater can not only facilitate the message, often it *is* the message. For example, the facilities at a Citibank or Bank of America, particularly the corporate offices and boardrooms, are intended to remind you of the size and power of these institutions. A key presentation by an advertising firm to a substantial prospective client may be equally dramatic—an impressive room, slides, catered food. Or, if it is thought that the client is looking for something more personal, the meeting might be informal and low-key, with the barest visual aids and the emphasis on the people. In a sense, in every meeting you're sell-

173

ing something: yourself, your product or service, an idea, an attitude, an environment. If you want a commitment, if you want your meeting partners to "buy" what you are selling, you should always attempt to establish a meeting environment that both conveys your message and complements your goal. When dealing with your own staff or others with whom you routinely meet, *do not* assume that this form of "selling" is unnecessary. In fact, the repetitive nature of the meeting may make your attention to the proper theater all the more important.

THEATER AND CONTROL

Because theater often works subliminally, it affords you an opportunity for control without the appearance of exercising control. The meeting room you choose, the clothes you wear, the language you use—all say something. It is not an accident that protocol is strictly observed in the deliberations of the United States Senate. When the clash of views is the basic business of the body, various theatrical rules (such as addressing each other as "my distinguished colleague") must be employed to remind participants that it is the principle rather than the person that is being debated. When you visit the boss's office, its size and decor remind you of his authority over you as well as his place in the company hierarchy.

Theater should not overwhelm the objective, otherwise it is poor theater. Like music in a film, theater should support the desired task. "If the music supports the action on screen without overwhelming it," says former Tri-Star Pictures Vice President of Music Tim Sexton, "it's an effective score. If I find myself concentrating on or criticizing the music, we've failed."

Recognizing the place of theater will assist you in removing the barriers to communication that cause meetings to fail. Using the techniques of theater will help you establish a mood, or circumstances, or inclinations that support what you want to accomplish.

KEY ELEMENTS OF THEATER

KNOW YOUR AUDIENCE

Your audience is the object of your theater. If you don't know what moves them, what bothers them, what motivates them, you have placed yourself at a serious disadvantage in using theater. It's like speaking in a foreign language.

Answering the following questions may help you focus on your audience:

1. Why are they at the meeting, and what do they want to accomplish?

2. What are their roles in relation to you? What are their impressions of you?

3. What "prejudices" do they have that affect them in this meeting?

4. What do you and they have in common?

5. What can you and they share that puts you and your audience on the same team?

Don't be afraid to ask questions about people with whom you will be meeting and whom you may not know. Learn about their companies, their jobs, their personal histories. Attempt to obtain a perspective on each person with whom you meet.

GET EARLY FAVORABLE REVIEWS

In nearly any meeting situation, but particularly those in which you are meeting for the first time, you will almost always be helped by favorable introductions of meeting participants, "early reviews" indicating the likelihood of success. These reviews break down barriers of communication and establish presumptions in your favor. So don't hesitate to ask for that phone call or letter of introduction before a critical meeting with a new person. Likewise, in presenting a new proposal to a familiar group, obtain favorable reviews from key members for the proposal prior to the meeting.

MUMMY, DUMMY, AND MERMIDON

Sometimes you can almost re-create your audience. Indianapolis attorney John Dillon used to bring part of his audience with him. Knowing that sheer numbers will influence the attitudes of other meeting members, Dillon used to bring secretaries, young associates, or other aides to certain kinds of meetings in which he envisioned a split vote beforehand. "You will be

Mummy, Dummy, and Mermidon," he would say to three new persons he might be initiating to the role. "I'll let you know when the time is right. Your job is to agree with me at different points in the meeting, to tell the group that it's a good idea or the right way to go." His team, like a laugh track for a TV comedy, would subliminally pull other participants Dillon's way.

THE GOOD COP/BAD COP GAME

Another common technique—not only in negotiation, but in other meetings as well—is the good cop/bad cop scenario. The good cop *appears* conciliatory and reasonable, the bad cop tough and irrational. In reality they are working on the same side, conspiring against you with the good cop placing himself in the position of reasonable middleman between "unreasonable you" and his unreasonable partner. The game may not even be intentional; some people at meetings are naturally conciliatory, others combative. You can play the same game by creating a "bad cop" on your side, someone with whom you purportedly must deal who is far tougher than you. Thus, you become the reasonable middleman, mediating a course of action between your own "unreasonable" partner and the unseen bad cop.

THE "OTHER AUDIENCE"

You often have an audience other than the one physically present at the meeting. The negotiator reports to his union, the manager to his supervisor, the principal to the school board. The union, the supervisor, and the school board may not be in the meeting with you, but they're in your meeting partners' heads, and that's just as important. Likewise, your position in future meetings is going to be affected by what they think. Every person at the meeting reflects his other audience, sometimes directly and sometimes without admitting it. Learn to look for these other audiences and beware the needs of your meeting partners in serving their demands.

COSTUME

There are still people who'll say, "Appearance shouldn't matter. It's what I am inside that really counts." The trouble is, people don't always have the time or opportunity to find out "who you really are." And even when they think it's worth their time, they still know that other people won't take the time. So the judgment they make about you is based not only on what *they* think, but on what they believe *others* think, since what others think will determine how effective you are in your business and professional life. Don't underestimate your appearance. You're trying to communicate, and almost the first communication you make is your physical appearance. What people see is what they think they are going to get.

What should you be trying to do with your appearance? First, don't change your *style*. You are who you are. But remember, you should also be trying to *remove barriers* to communication as well as *establish channels* of communication. You want to convey the qualities that will cause your meeting partners to listen. You want to convey qualities that are consistent with what you want to accomplish. Therefore, don't dress in a way that creates distrust or puts you on a different wavelength from your meeting partners.

When I was a young associate traveling to different parts of California to meet with clients who desired to form banks, I'd typically dress in a blue suit and dark tie. But while I seemed to be effective in meetings with clients in Los Angeles and San Francisco, the folks in Chino, a farming community east of Los Angeles, just didn't seem to want to hear what I had to say. The senior partner and I were heading back one day from Chino when he gave me some advice. "Look," he said, "next time dress down a bit. Wear a sport coat or one of your lighter suits. These people see you as a city slicker. They think you might think you're better than they are. There have been plenty of city slickers they don't like. I think if you look more 'regular,' they'll treat you more regular." He turned out to be right. They hadn't necessarily disliked me. But by wearing a dark, tailored suit, I became one of a dozen city types they thought they had met before and whom they didn't like.

People have quirks. Dr. Ernie Bates is a neurosurgeon, lecturer at the University of California Medical School, and chairman of American Shared Hospitals. He's in his late forties, open-minded, and seems to like all kinds of people. But he told me once very seriously, "I always look at the way a man dresses. His suit, his shirt, his tie. Is the suit pressed? Is he neat? But, in the

179

end, I look at his shoes. If he's got a nice suit and his shoes aren't polished, I know right away he's a phony. I always worry about a guy whose shoes aren't polished."

One person's shined shoes is another's class ring and another's concern over grammar. These are shorthand statements to other people, and you should try to make sure that you are giving off the signals you want them to hear. Pay attention to the theater of costume. Here's some simple advice on appearance:

1. Always be neat. Show care for your body and your clothes.

2. Generally dress a half step better than your meeting partners.

3. Take time to discover your own best styles and colors.

4. Stand erect and sit erect during the meeting.

THE SPIRIT OF PLACE

The lighting in nightclubs is soft and dark. Schoolrooms are well lit, with upright desks. Corporate boardrooms reflect power and authority. In each of these meetings the objectives are enhanced by the *spirit of place.*

A good imagination can work wonders, but don't underestimate the roles of location and setting in serving your purpose at any meeting. I've heard more than one person say something like "I can almost feel the knowledge seep in" as they walk through the Yard at Harvard University. Since they had been there just a few moments, it could only have been the spirit of place. People who visited the old Center for the Study of Democratic Institutions in Santa Barbara, California, have told me that the splendid surroundings actually made them think more clearly! An awareness of the past and responsibility for the future are inescapable in the Rotunda and the Senate and House chambers of the Capitol in Washington, D.C.

Different kinds of meetings require different locations. But the location is your playing field. Location tilts the action one way or another. It can help you or your opponent. It can reinforce chaos, feelings of negativity, and barriers to communication, or it can minimize them. Better yet, it can reflect order, positive feelings, and openness of communication.

YOUR OFFICE OR MINE?

There are three advantages to meeting in your own office. First, you can exercise a degree of control impossible elsewhere. You control access to the phone and other people and services. You will feel more comfortable. Your meeting partner will tend to defer.

There is an attorney is Los Angeles who enjoys keeping his office cool. Some years ago he noticed that other people were less comfortable than he was. Now, for difficult meetings, he turns the thermostat to about fifty-eight degrees. He knows that his greater tolerance gives him an advantage in meetings with adversaries —and he uses it. Of course, you don't have to get used to being cold. An attorney in my office recently kept the heat turned up in a negotiation session in his office when he learned that opposing counsel had not slept for two days. The opposing counsel wilted, literally and figuratively.

Second, meeting in your office offers you the opportunity to be a gracious host. As IMG's Mark McCormack says, "Simply by being polite and making the other person feel comfortable, you can diffuse [tension] and earn a certain amount of confidence and trust." You can also put yourself in a position where you are owed rather than owe. On the other hand, you can also show special courtesy on occasion by offering to meet in someone else's office.

Third, meeting in your offices will almost always save you time. The exception here is when you want to meet with a colleague in the same building. By meeting in his or her office you are in a position to leave when you want to leave.

However, don't insist on meeting in your office if by doing so you create tension—unless you want to create tension. And don't demand a meeting in your office when your meeting partner is clearly senior. In fact, you can score points by deferring to others when it is irrelevant to you or advisable to gain advantage.

RAISING EXPECTATIONS AND
PERFORMANCE THROUGH LOCATION

When I was first appointed by the governor of California to serve on the board of governors of the California Community Colleges, the board met in moderate-cost

hotel conference rooms in various locations throughout the state. The lighting was invariably poor, the microphones and other equipment seldom worked well,
and, as a whole, the impression created for both the
fifteen-member board and the audience attending the
meetings was mediocre at best. The board had over-
sight responsibility for the nearly $1.5 billion spent
annually on California's community colleges, but its
actual authority was confusing. Myriad local boards,
administrator and faculty organizations, an accrediting
agency, and the state legislature itself fractionalized
power and authority. What was desired most of the
board of governors was leadership, but without corre-
sponding authority that's a chicken-and-egg problem.
While it was only a small piece in the puzzle, I was
convinced that the board's stature and self-image, and
therefore its dialogue and decisions, could be enhanced by a change in the location of its meetings.

For a short time board members fought a change in
location, believing that to upgrade the meeting facility
would be to admit implicitly a weakness for irrelevant
stimuli or to risk being perceived as elitist. But after a
few weeks of lobbying, the board voted to seek a new
meeting location, and I was given the task of choosing
the place. With a necessary deference to the legislature, which still had great control over the community
colleges, I decided we should begin meeting in one of
the ornate and majestic senate hearing rooms of the
State Capitol Building. With some members grum-
bling, we tried it. After initial self-consciousness,
members sat straighter in their chairs, discussion became more civil and thoughtful, testimony from others

became more concise and informed, and the board demanded more—and got more—from the staff. Over time, the public perception of the board meetings changed, and the board's perception of itself changed —due in no small part, I believe, to the spirit of our new meeting place.

In all your meetings, but particularly your routine meetings, give thought to location. Think about the comfort of your meeting partners, the image you want to convey, and what advantages you are creating for yourself. Ask yourself what feelings you want in order to meet your purpose. Then ask how the location can help you create those feelings.

THE SIZE AND KIND OF ROOM

The size of your meeting room obviously facilitates comfort, but in certain kinds of meetings it also sends a message: Is this meeting a success? For business entertaining, generally pick a room that will be a little smaller than you might really require. Never pick a room that is larger than you require. It will look as if fewer people came than expected; that is, as if expectations were not met. A smaller room will make the affair *look* like a success and will create the energy and intensity necessary for those types of meetings. On the other hand, where real work is required over a period of time, your major concerns should be comfort and communication.

The kind of room and the facilities you select are equally important. If you're considering a business lunch, make sure it meets the expectations of your meeting partner and the image you want to convey. If it's a working lunch with your staff, make sure there is room enough for any paperwork. Make sure, too, that you have enough privacy and that you'll all be able to hear each other. Don't crowd people into your office, with papers on laps, and expect to get maximum results. As the person who has scheduled the meeting room, you have responsibility for these decisions. You are making a statement about your ability to manage people, even if you've assigned the task to somebody else.

SEATING

As a then-member of the U.S. Attorney's Office in Los Angeles, California, Attorney General John Van de Kamp was invited to meet with famed FBI chief J. Edgar Hoover in Washington. "I entered Hoover's office and was asked to take a seat on a couch that was no more than a foot off the ground and was so cushy that, in sitting, I sank nearly to the floor. By contrast, Hoover was seated in an oversized chair on a raised platform behind the desk. I felt I was put in a physical position to do nothing but listen to the master. Everything made me want to say 'yes.' Happily, he didn't ask for anything. Later in the meeting, a number of field agents filed in for a few moments. There was Hoover, greeting them on a raised area of the floor while they filed past him below. It was incredible!"

Seating can have a profound impact on behavior in

any meeting. Don't overdo, but be aware of the environment you're creating by virtue of seating arrangements.

DESK OR COUCH?

Remaining behind your desk puts a barrier between you and your meeting partner. It gives you a place to write and keep notes while he must fumble with his papers in a chair. You have access to the phone, he doesn't. For most meetings, the position behind the desk is a control position. And that's often the position in which you want to be. But if you want to make someone feel comfortable, or if the person with whom you are meeting demands, by his stature, force of personality, or position, treatment as a peer or a superior, move to a more comfortable seating area of your office or a conference room table, where you can address each other on an equal basis. When dealing with subordinates, you're more likely to get candid advice or elicit new ideas when your meeting partner is not reminded of his vulnerability. Put a coffeepot on the table and offer to pour a cup, and you've made a greater gesture of warmth and hospitality still. Serve lunch, and you've said the conversation can and should go beyond business. When you're in a position of equality, try to go out of your way to be courteous. You achieve an implicit IOU.

If you are dealing with a peer who demands meeting in his office and remains behind his desk, you can diminish his control in shorter meetings by remaining standing and pacing the room. You gain a height advantage, and his eyes must follow you. Within a couple of minutes you'll find him standing too.

THINK ABOUT WHO'S NEXT TO WHOM

In any meeting, judgments about seating can sometimes make or break a particular purpose and make or break your reputation. Think about seating first from your perspective. Then put yourself in each of the other seats and look at the meeting from that person's perspective.

Los Angeles Chamber of Commerce President Ray Remy relates a story that took place when he served as deputy mayor of Los Angeles (the second-highest-ranking position in the city) and still makes him shake with rage. The city of Los Angeles wanted to develop better relations with the White House in the first years of the Reagan administration. A dinner meeting was to be arranged by the city's lobbyist in Washington so that a high-ranking White House official could join Remy and some members of the city council in an effort to get things moving better. Everyone other than Remy was meeting the White House official, a very conservative Republican, for the first time. Remy was an old friend.

"So," Remy says, "the lobbyist, who works for both the council and the mayor's office, seats the very conservative White House official between Councilman David Cunningham and Bob Farrell, both of whom are no-holds-barred liberals. He wants to make them feel important. Then he sits another liberal councilman across from this very conservative White House guy.

187

Presumably he thought it would make for an interesting dialogue. Then he seats me at the far end of the table, too far away to carry on any conversation with the guy. Now here we are. The purpose of the dinner is to *try to develop a better relationship.* It was definitely not to change anybody's mind on anything. What it succeeded in doing was making the White House person very uncomfortable, since he was forced to defend Reagan policy all night, and it made Bob and David a little mad at what they could see coming out of the Reagan administration. So we established a relationship all right—a lousy one! And it made me furious. After the debacle, I told the guy's boss I'd never be involved with the guy again because of the lack of judgment he showed simply in doing the seating for this dinner."

MEETING FACE TO FACE

Whatever the prevailing mood, it will be *intensified* when meeting face to face, particularly in large groups. The energy is focused right back at the other party. A meeting of persons in a full circle is more intense still. This is neither good nor bad per se. It depends upon what you are trying to accomplish. If control is of importance, such a seating arrangement makes control more difficult since all of the parties attain equal status and tend to respond to the persons across from them and not to the leader. On the other hand, discussion itself can be creative and intense. Semicircles tend to be good for problem-solving meetings because while most people can see everyone else, they can also focus on the discussion leader. A semi-circle also affords more control for the leader.

LONG TABLES

Long tables are wonderful *control* mechanisms that otherwise possess great limitations. Since the members have great difficulty seeing those on the same side of the table, discussion among them will be limited. Everyone feels a little "out of it"; that is, they tend to believe they are missing something and therefore hesitate to participate. When they do participate, they will tend to overreact to those across from them. Often the best way to deal with two allied troublemakers is to put them a few seats away from each other on the same side of the table, where communication is difficult and their effectiveness is minimized.

ASSIGNED SEATING

In formal meetings, consider using assigned seating to accomplish your goals with respect to individual participants and your overall purpose. In informal meetings, consider something just short of assigned seating. Think of the two most critical participants. One may be a valuable team player, one may be a troublemaker. Think about where you want them in relation to you. Then simply say, "John, why don't you sit next to me here, and Bill, why don't you take the seat at the end of the table." In ten seconds of conversation, you may have made your meeting a great deal easier.

"ORDAINED" SEATING

At my second meeting of the board of regents of the University of California, some of us watched with near horror as one of the other new regents flopped himself down in what for some thirty years had been Carter Hawley Hale founder Ed Carter's established seat just to the left of the president of the university. Carter soon entered the room with the president, and they moved slowly toward the head of the board table. Their conversation continued as they stood behind their traditional seats. Three long minutes passed. Finally, with others looking over nervously, the new member got the point: there was no assigned seating per se, but he was in the wrong seat.

The boss may have a traditional place at the meeting table. Or a group that meets regularly may have established tacitly assigned seating. Be careful before you sit down that there are not tacit arrangements that dictate where you should *not* sit.

SEATING WITH REFERENCE TO
OTHER POWER SOURCES

Be aware who the other sources of influence are at the meeting and position yourself so that you can make eye contact easily. In fact, as a general rule, the more people with whom you can make direct and easy eye contact during a meeting, the more control you will have.

Where you choose to sit should depend upon your

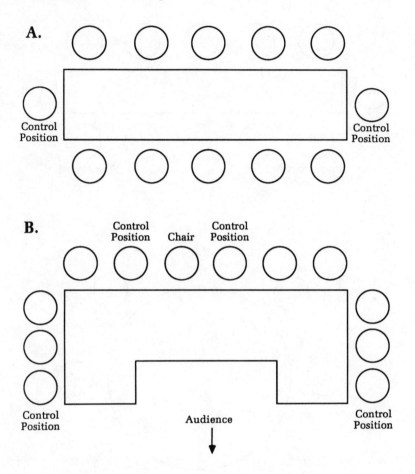

A.

Control Position

Control Position

B.

Control Position   Chair   Control Position

Control Position

Control Position

Audience

own purpose. If you want to be uninvolved for some reason, pick the seating position that permits you to be. If you're seeking to win your point, or if you want the option of seizing control when you believe it is in your interest to do so, pick one of the controlling positions. Diagrams A and B note where the control positions are in various seating arrangements. Diagrams C

191

C.

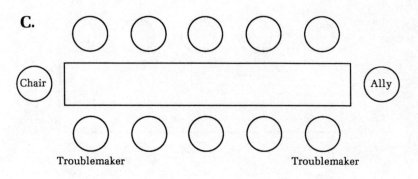

D.

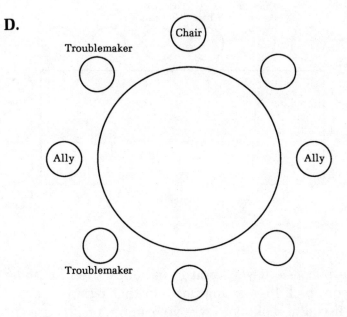

and D note the seating arrangements that can consolidate your control by positioning your allies and isolating the troublemakers.

SEATING AND BRAINSTORMING

Brainstorming will be enhanced when barriers to communication are broken down. In brainstorming, you want ideas. Therefore, you want people to feel comfortable offering what sometimes may appear to be silly ideas. Seating arrangements that make people feel comfortable, remove signs of status, and treat participants as "equals" work better than those that constantly remind participants who's the boss. This is more difficult than you may think, since meetings by their nature are status arenas in which authority is maintained and judged. Long tables are horrible for brainstorming. Circles are intense. Semicircles present a good balance of control and creativity.

LOOK OUT FOR YOUR OWN BIASES

I used to practice law with a partner who would call departmental meetings from time to time to talk about legal problems. He had the unfortunate habit of focusing on his then most favored employee, no matter where the person sat. He would then direct most of his comments and statements at that employee, disregarding the rest of the group, which would feel smaller and smaller and contribute less and less. Be conscious of whom you tend to relate to. If necessary, put powerful meeting partners in weaker meeting positions and weaker meeting partners in strong positions when dealing with subordinates.

THE MIDDLE BLOCK

Nearly thirty years ago, Professor C. Northcote Parkinson called attention to the "Middle Block" in a meeting, the members of which include "those who cannot hear what is being said and those who cannot understand even if they did. To secure their votes, what is needed is primarily the example of others voting on either side of them." When possible, put those who are by nature followers in a position to be influenced during the meeting by those who are your supporters or whose judgment you respect. Isolate your opponents in positions where their influence over others is minimized.

PROPS

All theater is aided by props. Charts and graphs can often communicate trends better than a single paragraph. But remember, too, that props can cause meeting partners to disassociate from the underlying task and focus on the quality of the prop. Thus, props can be as disruptive to group thought as they can be helpful. I once had a business associate who always brought a prop of some kind to a meeting in which he was on the spot. It might have nothing to do with the meeting at hand. He was the first person I knew to get hold of the official pins for the 1984 Olympics. At one meeting he began by giving everyone a pin—very much in demand—and he succeeded in distracting

194

the group from an issue boiling just under the surface.

Consider using audiovisual aids to assist in getting your point across. We tend to feel as much as we think. When dealing with any group, concepts are easily misunderstood or *not* understood. The skillful use of audiovisual aids can really help, and they can keep people stimulated. In using such aids, consider the following:

1. *If at all possible, rehearse.* The power of audiovisual aids is such that if you use them poorly, the damage is worse than if you don't use them at all. Also, make sure that someone is responsible for the proper functioning of all equipment, including microphones.

2. *Focus.* We tend to remember twenty percent of what we hear, thirty percent of what we see, and fifty percent of what we hear *and* see. Use your props only for major points and key concepts. If you use props for minor points, they will gain unintended significance.

3. *Quality.* Any time you use a prop, you equate it with you and your company or organization in the minds of your meeting partners. Make sure its quality and taste reflect well upon you.

4. *Brevity.* Don't overdo the use of visual aids or any other props. You'll lose impact.

5. *Almost anything is a potential prop.* Your watch, your pen, a piece of art in your office—all of these are props, too. They convince, distract, and entertain. They make a statement. If you remain aware, you can use the things around you to break the ice or make a point. Props can make you, and therefore your meetings, interesting.

ON BEHALF OF THEATER

Do not confuse good theater with histrionics or show-boating. Most of the time, good theater is unobtrusive. It should subtly influence meetings—and it usually does. Its impact is always there. The next time you walk into someone's office, ask yourself what relationships he has established and what feelings he has created by virtue of its size, decor, desk alignment, and comfort. The next time you're at a staff meeting, note where people sit and see if it doesn't influence their roles. Watch the quiet, apparently unassuming meeting master, the one who seems to have no airs, and see if he hasn't developed a meeting theater that suits his goal. Work to make your meetings stimulating and your partners interested and interesting. Use the techniques of theater to enhance your objective; eliminate the theater that undermines it.

CHAPTER THIRTEEN
Using the Cast of Characters

HAVE PATIENCE WITH THE JEALOUSIES AND PETU-
LANCES OF ACTORS, FOR THEIR HOUR IS THEIR
ETERNITY.

—Richard Garrett

IN your meetings, you may choose to assign the job of
note taker to one person or discussion leader to another, but in general your meeting partners will assume other roles naturally. Some appear to be villains,
and some appear to be heroes. More often than not
they are simply responding to the other people at the
meeting and the issues under discussion in a manner
consistent with their basic personalities and needs.
You cannot change personalities and basic needs, and
you shouldn't expect to. But with a certain amount of
patience and with the recognition that your own actions may appear to others to be equally peculiar, you
can encourage the cast of characters at any meeting to
work for you.

You won't find the following characters at every
meeting. And sometimes you'll see different characters in the same person. But look for these predomi-

nant tendencies, and try to play to their strengths and use them to your advantage.

THE GOOD GUYS

THE INITIATOR

He has initiative and imagination. He gets things started. He can offer ideas and solutions. He gets a charge out of being the first one out of the gate. But he can have a large ego and requires recognition for what he contributes. Learn to look to him for ideas and give him credit. Don't come down on him publicly for lack of follow-through if he's weak in that area. Try to involve him early on any issue. Think of him as the right side of your brain, the creative, intuitive side.

THE ORIENTER

He can refocus the attention of the group. Not as creative as the initiator, he is less likely to be taken off track by the excitement of new ideas. His weakness is his failure to explore. Approach him before the meeting regarding what you want to accomplish; he can be your navigator.

THE FACILITATOR

He clarifies without offending. He asks questions and distinguishes arguments. He can have trouble coming to a decision but is very capable of interpreting and restating the group position. Don't look to him too early, for he may facilitate before any conflict has materialized. Look to him when there is a deadlock.

THE RECONCILER

Like the facilitator, he is often older and wiser than other meeting partners. He seems to have been around the block. He can reduce tension with a joke or perspective. Make sure he's involved and appreciated.

THE SUPPORTER

He is a supportive personality with a word of encouragement for all, though not necessarily a leader. He finds what's positive about a statement. He may have trouble with hard choices. Unless he seeks responsibility, don't burden him; he's a supporter because that's what he's comfortable doing.

THE BAD GUYS

THE AGGRESSOR

He questions everything, criticizes ideas, and attacks people personally. He wants attention and can't get it through other means. He sees problems but seldom offers solutions. Give him the attention he requires early on. If he's made part of the process, he is less likely to criticize. During the meeting, seat him next to a strong ally if you possibly can.

THE PLAYBOY

This character tries to show his disinterest in the meeting. He engages in side discussions, reads other materials, and generally attempts to remain uninvolved. He is usually harmless unless he also has tendencies of the aggressor, in which case treat him as you would the aggressor. Basically he wants attention; find interests in common with him that do not necessarily relate to the meeting.

MR. KNOW-IT-ALL

He thinks he knows everything. He manipulates conversation and seeks control. Sometimes he knows quite a bit; sometimes he doesn't. If he's confronted directly in the meeting, he'll often only get worse. He, too, is best controlled by getting him involved, seeking his advice prior to the meeting. Also, try to establish a meeting process in general that affords equal time to others so that you do not have to play the heavy.

SOCIAL LEADERS/PROCESS LEADERS

Some people tend to be social leaders in meetings, others tend to be process leaders. Social people deal in terms of people rather than issues or process. They naturally converse before and after the meeting with other meeting partners. They are sensitive to the feelings and emotions of others. They enjoy the human contact in meetings. They are often humorous. Most of all, they are interested in relating to other people.

Process people look for order. They naturally distinguish process from substance and are equally concerned with each, but they are less likely to be good with people in a meeting environment. They are quick to focus and quick to notice when the discussion goes off track. But they may or may not have the personal skills to retrieve it.

Most meetings require both social and process leadership. Sometimes the same person will have both qualities. More often each person requires help in one or the other area. Assess your own tendencies and learn to look to others to fill the vacuum. If you're a process leader, your best ally is probably the social leader. If you're a social leader, recognize that you need the help of someone skilled in process.

REDUCING TENSION WITH HUMOR

People are human and there's bound to be tension in some meetings. One of the best ways to release such tension is through humor. In fact, there is now medical evidence that a good laugh actually lowers the pulse rate. The deeper the laugh, the greater the effect. A real knee slapper can reduce the pulse rate for up to forty-five minutes and can thereby reduce stress and tension among the participants. If you see tension building among your cast of characters, deal with it as early as you can. In some situations, you may even wish to call attention to the potential for discord and

201

make the other participants responsible for dealing with it. But humor, properly timed, is often the best antidote for tension and stress.

PLAYING TO STRENGTH

In general, you get the most out of the cast of characters at any meeting by providing the positive attention they require and making use of their strengths. With groups of subordinates, you won't want the "bad guys" around too long. Unfortunately, they are less likely to act their roles with a superior. It is their peers and subordinates who must suffer. As peers, these "bad guys" often represent outside interests (such as groups of similar employees or persons with similar interests), and therefore their input is important no matter how obnoxious they may seem. Try to separate what they are saying from the person who is saying it. As co-workers, of course, you have to live with them. Since basic needs and insecurities are always stronger than any particular view on any particular issue, seek to establish a relationship with co-workers that serves those needs outside the meeting. Be supportive of the person and you'll find him more supportive of you in your meetings.

Of course, when you have a choice about the participants, you should eliminate the "bad guys" from the meeting whenever you can. Those whom you can't eliminate you must treat with the same respect you would show your most valued participants.

CHAPTER FOURTEEN
Your Most Powerful Weapon— The Agenda

THE SPOKEN WORD PERISHES; THE WRITTEN WORD REMAINS.

—Latin proverb

EVERY lawyer knows what a tremendous advantage it is to prepare the first draft of a legal agreement. Everything—every point, every detail—can be drafted in his client's favor. Issues given away in the third paragraph can be subtly taken back in the thirteenth paragraph. A well-drafted legal agreement puts the opposing counsel in an awkward position from the very beginning, and it requires an experienced opponent to work hard to regain even ground, let alone the advantage.

Likewise, he who controls the agenda controls the meeting. It's better than the first draft of a legal agreement. It reflects the presumptive skeleton of the minutes and therefore suggests the results. It sets forth whose issues will be discussed and in what order. It legitimates certain issues and makes others illegitimate. In fact, a written agenda becomes almost law to meeting participants. When you're the one leading a meeting, you owe it to yourself (and, if you want their help, your meeting partners) to have prepared and circulated an agenda. The meeting masters in your group will expect it. When you're the one attending a meeting, you ought to make clear that you require an agenda in advance; otherwise someone is either incompetent or out to take advantage of you.

THE AGENDA AS ROAD MAP

Every meeting should have an agenda, and in more meetings than not that agenda should be written and circulated before the meeting. There is a tendency to avoid preparing a written agenda. But while certain circumstances preclude working from a written agenda, or the routine nature of a meeting has so firmly fixed the agenda in the minds of the participants that a written agenda is unnecessary, discarding a written agenda should be the exception rather than the rule.

If an agenda were a mere shopping list of items to cover, its importance would be far less than it otherwise is. But an agenda is more than a shopping list. It is the construction or plan for the meeting, the most valuable tool in keeping the group mind focused in order to achieve the desired objective. When it's written, it's there for everyone to refer to. You don't have to remind people—the agenda, that neutral third party, says so.

Like architectural plans for a house, even the exercise of drawing up the agenda is itself critical to creating the shape of the meeting. The meeting will have to proceed in a particular order to ensure that its objectives are met. The agenda should help the participants in understanding what is expected of them each step of the way.

There are four distinct roles performed by an agenda. First, it is a tool to help you prepare for the meeting. Second, it communicates to participants in advance what is to be considered and what is expected of them. Third, it is a script for the meeting itself, a mechanism for order and control. And fourth, it is a standard by which the success or failure of the meeting can be measured.

THE AGENDA AS CRYSTAL BALL

The agenda is really not a crystal ball, but its preparation can focus your visualization of the meeting so that you are more likely to accomplish your objective. In preparing an agenda, make a list of the different objectives you want to accomplish reflected in the "items." Then play through in your own mind the likely responses or contributions of your participants with respect to each item. This will help you see what steps may be necessary to take even before the meeting. Certainly you cannot know what every person will say, but you should know something about their relationship with you, their background and aspirations, their interests and objectives, so that you can make reasonable estimations of their positions or the kinds of things they're going to contribute or be concerned about at the meeting. Then you can determine to provide additional information or meet separately with certain participants in advance. You can also eliminate items that conflict or whose objectives are unattainable under the circumstances. You can order the items for maximum impact. And you can add items for cosmetic purposes if you think it necessary.

Using the agenda in this way is no less useful for meetings with your subordinates than it is when you're negotiating a deal. The minute or so it takes you to draft an agenda for a meeting with your subordinates will help you conduct a better-structured, shorter meeting, as well as achieve the desired results.

THE AGENDA AS REALITY

Written agendas give a special air of legitimacy and purpose to a meeting. If I tell you over the phone what our agenda is and repeat it at the beginning of the meeting, it has not nearly the same weight as a full, detailed, written agenda circulated in advance. Participants will almost always wander mentally in and out of the meeting. Each time they return, the agenda will remind them what the meeting is about, where the group is, and where it's going. People tend to think that if it's in writing, it must be true. The written agenda becomes reality.

In fact, the power of a written agenda is so strong that during the meeting the participants often feel the need to ask others to write down new items on the agenda in order to legitimize them! That tells you not only how "real" the written agenda becomes, but also the heavy burden placed on others when they seek to change the agenda. That's control.

When properly crafted, a good agenda can also facilitate discussion, keep things in order, and move the meeting along—for everyone's benefit. Drafting such an agenda usually requires some consultation with participants in advance. And as both a leader and participant, every effort should be made to *follow* the agenda for maximum results.

An Iron Fist in a Velvet Glove

The agenda is a relatively short document, but it can reference reports, policy statements, and future actions with far-reaching effects. It can have far more significance than its one or two pages may indicate. For the skilled meeting leader the agenda is an important weapon because he doesn't allow anything on it that doesn't serve his own interests. The agenda you prepare should serve exactly the same purpose.

THE DISGUISED AGENDA

Agendas don't have to look like agendas to be either helpful or dangerous. A document submitted to a group for approval may contain items that are routinely accepted in context; but if highlighted in an agenda, these same items might engender debate.

A number of years ago I got a call from the new owner of a small music-publishing company. He was about to meet and discuss entering into a deal with a songwriter and asked me for advice. The songwriter had a reputation for being a little unreliable, and the publisher wanted me to draw up a tough contract. He had scheduled a meeting to discuss "deal points" with the songwriter and asked me, "Other than the obvious financial terms, what key points should be on the agenda for this meeting?"

I told him he needed only one item. "Tell him that rather than having your own agenda, you're willing to accept the Standard Form Songwriters Agreement," I said. "Tell him you don't want anything special. I can give you a copy of the form used by the major publishing companies. It's marked 'Standard Form' and has all you need. Just don't change it." They met, they talked for a while, and the songwriter signed the agreement. The Standard Form was less threatening than a personal agenda but actually contained in entirety the publisher's real agenda.

HOW TO RIG THE AGENDA

Most people are a little lazy. If you're willing to supply an agenda and plan of action, it's likely to be the legitimate starting and ending point of any meeting. Recently Dr. Walter Kohn, a nationally known physicist, captured a meeting he wasn't chairing by circulating in advance a proposed course of action. Since no one else presented a written agenda, let alone a proposal, his proposal became the agenda. Meetings abhor a vacuum; that's what makes them risky. Dr. Kohn filled the vacuum. His proposal didn't look like an agenda, but it not only covered several *different* issues, in his *preferred order*, it also directed *follow-up*. His proposal made sense. It was a benevolent wolf in sheep's clothing, but a wolf nonetheless. Now, you might say that if the course of action made so much sense, it probably would have been adopted in any event. Maybe, but not necessarily. Kohn is an influential fellow. People tend to mix the position with the person. Had his position not been known early on, meeting members might have taken opposing positions. But since Kohn's position was clear very early, members felt opposition to his *position* was also opposition to *Kohn*. Of course, if the village idiot comes out with his position first, the meeting feels pressure the other way.

In rigging an agenda:

1. Draft the agenda with the minutes in mind.

2. If someone else is preparing the agenda, make sure your item is on the agenda.

3. Make sure your item is early enough on the agenda so that the group gets to it.

4. Your key item should not be first on the agenda, since the group generally focuses too much attention on the earliest issues and is often overly critical.

5. Contact key allies before the meeting. If appropriate, have your ally speak to your item first.

The art of preparing an effective agenda is most critical in formal meetings, such as those of regularly scheduled boards, commissions, clubs, or other organizations. But the rules that apply to formal agendas ought to be considered even in the most informal meetings. It is useful to at least have considered the points that follow.

DON'T CONFUSE A BRIEF AGENDA WITH A BRIEF MEETING

Bringing brevity to meetings is often a problem; bringing brevity to the agenda is not. The more serious problem is that agendas tend to be too brief and too vague. This is not to encourage you to pile on more *items!* On the contrary, you should always limit the number of items. But if you've already determined that an item deserves a place on the meeting agenda and cannot be better handled by some other tool, you must tell your meeting partners enough about it to make their contributions meaningful. The tendency is simply to list the topics to be discussed without further elaboration, telling the participant almost nothing. This is the laundry-list approach. Instead, each item should tell the participant enough to allow him or her to do any necessary preparation and to understand what you hope to achieve through consideration of the item. An agenda will usually call for different types of tasks. You must at least tell participants whether a particular item is for information, discussion, action, or all three. Meetings fail because participants are not clear about what is on the table at a particular moment and what is ultimately expected. Let them know so that they can direct their preparations and contributions accordingly.

Here's an example of a typical agenda distributed in advance for an organization:

1. Minutes
2. President's Remarks
3. 1988 Budget (to be distributed)
4. Conference Report
5. Committee Reports
   a. Finance
   b. Long-Range Planning
6. New Business
7. Adjourn

Here's how the agenda, distributed in advance, might have been better prepared:

1. <u>Minutes</u>: Approval of minutes of meeting of January 15, 1986. This is an ACTION ITEM. Minutes attached.
2. <u>President's Remarks</u>: DISCUSSION ONLY. Report attached.
3. <u>Budget for 1988</u>: ACTION ITEM. BUDGET INCLUDED IN MATERIALS. The 1988 budget was approved by the Finance Committee at the December meeting. Action by the full group was deferred at the December meeting pending only receipt of a staff report regarding the MacArthur Program, appearing on page 8. The staff report, preceded by an executive summary, is enclosed for your review. Staff recommends approval.
4. <u>Report on Conferences</u>: DISCUSSION ONLY. At its October meeting, we requested a report by staff enu-

merating the various conferences to which we are invited to send a representative and an analysis of the strengths and weaknesses of particular conferences. The report is attached. It is the intention of the President to recommend action at the *next* meeting.

5. Committee Reports:
   a) Finance Committee: ACTION ITEM. The report of the committee is attached. Recommended actions appear on page 1 of the report.
   b) Long-Range Planning: A *draft* report is attached *for discussion*. The final report is expected to be approved by committee at its meeting *in two months*.
6. New Business.
7. Adjournment.

GET THE AGENDA OUT EARLY

Once prepared, the agenda should be circulated far enough in advance to allow review by participants. They may want to do a little homework. But it should not be distributed so far in advance that it will be laid aside, unless you intend to send out another copy later. Of course, there are times when you'll want to surprise an opponent with an agenda, not giving him enough time to change it. But in any event, always bring extra copies to the meeting. It's your agenda and to your advantage to have it in front of your meeting partners.

ROUTINE MEETINGS

University of California President David Gardner describes the agenda-setting process for his routine meetings as follows:

> I have a weekly meeting with all my vice presidents and my immediate staff all in one room usually for an hour to an hour and one-half. This is every Monday. An agenda is circulated Thursday prior to the Monday. I put items on the agenda, and one of my staff reaches each of the others to determine if they have items they want on the agenda. I make the final decision of what goes on the agenda, but part of my purpose is to get to what may be on the minds of others as well as what is appropriate for all to hear. Also, having the agenda distributed in advance gives them the opportunity to seek the advice and counsel of their own staffs, since by necessity they may not be informed on all of the issues. It would be a waste of time to bring the issue up and either discuss it without appropriate preparation or continually defer the matter to a later meeting. On the other hand, if I determine that we are not prepared for an item because of the nature of the issue or some other reason, I cancel the item from the agenda. I don't want us to waste time. And I want to create the sense that when we do have a meeting, an item is important and deserves the attention of the meeting participants.

SET TIME LIMITS

Indicate the time when the meeting will begin and when you expect it to end. To the greatest extent possible, stick to those time constraints. Work will expand to fill the time available. You can always relax the schedule, but you need something to relax. Also, try to estimate the time to be spent on *each item* of the agenda. Note it on the agenda whenever practicable. Again, you can always be flexible if flexibility is needed. For the routine items, follow your proposed time schedule closely. This is where time is often wasted with trivial discussion. When a particular item requires more time, take it.

People tend to talk about what they know and understand, and they tend to avoid what they don't know and cannot comprehend. You can help overcome this tendency by scheduling items largely in order of their relative importance, both to the organization and to you personally.

THE EXECUTIVE SUMMARY

Says Los Angeles Chamber of Commerce President Ray Remy, "It used to be very frustrating to me, when I was a young staff person, to see elected officials and others come to meetings and thumb through the sheaf of materials that we had carefully prepared. Here they were at the meeting, and they clearly hadn't read the materials we had spent so much time putting together. I *used* to think, How do these people function as effective policy makers? Of course now that I attend these same types of meetings as a principal myself, I embarrassingly find myself at the meeting clumsily thumbing through these voluminous reports I haven't read! The truth is that I don't have time to get through all that material. As a policy maker I find I need concise, accurate statements with respect to the problem being addressed and clear options to solve problems already identified. If I want more information on a particular issue, I want it available. But I don't want to have to sort through a massive amount of material, some of which may be policy, some detail, some background. Some sort of executive summary is critical."

An "executive summary" is not necessary, of course, for all meetings. But whenever the material is more than three pages in length, an executive summary can amplify the particular agenda items, summarize reports, and clarify what is expected of policy makers. You should always *consider*, therefore, whether an executive summary of the item is appropriate. Some people make the error of assuming that an executive summary is some kind of an insult to intelligence. Actually, however, the more sophisticated the meeting partners and the more their role is devoted to policy formation, the more they will be used to and expect executive summaries. It is not because they can't read. It is because they know and accept the limits of their role and their time.

OTHER PAPER AT THE MEETING

Papers distributed at the meeting are of little use unless very brief—no more than one page. Time and again you'll see someone passing out a report at the meeting with the obvious expectation that it will be seriously considered. It won't be. In fact, it will distract from discussion. Nor will it be read afterward unless some later action is required. Distributing such reports at the meeting may allow you to bluff something through if you're agile enough. Or it may make you feel good. It may even impress some of the lightweight members of the group. But the sophisticated meeting manager will immediately suspect that you are either late preparing the material, trying to sneak something through, or unable to handle a meeting.

Any paper distributed at a meeting will immediately attract the attention of the group, if only to look at the pictures. It distracts from the chair and the presentation. It shifts the focus away from the issue at hand and onto the medium. Background papers and reports of any length, in particular, should be distributed in advance. If you find yourself putting them before the meeting at the last minute, you're probably making a mistake.

STRUCTURING DISCUSSION IN AN AGENDA

LIMBERING UP

Just as the human body takes some time to warm up and any team takes a few plays to get on track, a meeting requires some early limbering up. By telling a joke or presenting an easy issue, you pull the group into the game. Get announcements out of the way quickly and move through an easy issue first. Your group will then begin to generate a winner's momentum.

ENERGY

As a general rule, energy dissipates as the meeting progresses. Therefore, if you are looking for a contribution from your meeting partners, it is usually best to consider the most demanding issues earlier in the meeting rather than later. On the other hand, if you are looking not for contributions but simply to have your way, it may be more appropriate to allow your meeting partners to expend their energy on the less important items, develop a railroad attitude, and then as time dwindles push your big item through.

FIRST ITEM AND LAST ITEM

Your meetings should begin and end on positive notes. Beginning the meeting with an item you feel can be completed successfully sets up the expectation of success for the entire meeting. That positive attitude and the momentum created can be very helpful later. Likewise, when participants leave you want them to feel it was a good meeting. Try to end with an item or issue that makes people feel they have accomplished something. If you can't do that, as chair or participant you can summarize what came out of the meeting that was positive.

USING THE AGENDA TO MOVE FORWARD TO ACTION

There is a logical and necessary order of discussion with respect to most actions taken in a meeting. If you state the questions in the proper order for consideration, and if you explain the steps that have preceded the action currently contemplated, you are more likely to keep discussion on track. As a guide, once you've determined what *purpose* is being served by *each agenda item* (that is, information exchange, isolation of the problem, idea generation, decision making, delegation, and so on), ask yourself whether it will be clear in the minds of the meeting participants how you got to where you are. If it's the least bit unclear, allow the agenda and supporting material to bring the participants up to date.

For example, instead of merely noting "Report of Accountant Selection Committee" in the agenda, consider the following substitute:

> *Report of Accountant Selection Committee.* (Discussion only.) By order of the board August 10, 1986, a committee was formed to conduct a search and recommend a new outside accounting firm for the company.

The committee was to report its recommendation to the board for *discussion only* at this meeting. Actual selection by the board is to be made at the next meeting. The committee has met on several occasions. The report containing its recommendation is attached for your review and discussion.

To sum up, if you're going into a meeting without a formal agenda, you've probably left your most effective weapon behind. The agenda in your head must now compete on an even footing with (1) everyone else's vague perception of the agenda for the meeting; (2) every single personal agenda; and (3) every distraction and every off road the discussion takes. The job of making the meeting do what it's supposed to do becomes that much harder. Force yourself to utilize a written agenda. It will be viewed not as a sign of weakness but as a sign of experience, wisdom, and strength.

CHAPTER FIFTEEN

The Order of Discussion: Rome Wasn't Built in a Day

THE SHORTEST WAY TO DO MANY THINGS IS TO
DO ONLY ONE THING AT A TIME.

—Richard Cecil

As we have seen, the "group mind" has great difficulty in following a line of thought. When a particular task is being pursued in a meeting—for instance, information sharing—it's tough enough. But when a meeting takes on an entire series of tasks, the job is more difficult still. Most discussions implicitly involve many tasks in order to reach a conclusion. Different tasks require somewhat different processes. Exercise patience. You can't have an effective discussion by approaching all the tasks, the problems, and the people at the same time. You've got to distinguish the tasks, separate the process from the substance, and separate the people from the problems.

SEPARATE PROCESS FROM SUBSTANCE

The question "how to decide" is different from "what to decide," although "how" will always influence "what." Prior to addressing substantive issues at a meeting, a group should know what the process will be for making a decision. For instance, will all solutions be presented before discussing any? Will we choose one or recommend three? Will the decision be made by consensus? By majority rule? By the chair after consultation with the group? Who has decided or will decide the criteria by which the decision will be made?

These are process questions that are best addressed early. Once substantive considerations are on the table, members will tend to seek the process that supports their substantive advantages or benefits. Of course, you should envision process questions when you prepare for the meeting. If you have a substantive goal, you should early on be pushing the process that will assist in achieving your goal.

For example, assume there are five proposals that will be under consideration at a nine-member committee meeting. Going in, you've counted the votes: your proposal has two votes (including yours), Bill's proposal has four votes, and the three other proposals have one vote each. The chair has not decided. You have also learned that those who are supporting the other proposals don't care for Bill's proposal at all.

Under this scenario, it is likely that the decision the

group reaches will depend largely on process. If there is to be discussion and then a vote on all proposals simultaneously, Bill's proposal will win since it has the plurality of votes. However, if the process calls for selecting the top two proposals and then voting, your proposal will triumph. If you are out to win your point of view, you should see all this before the meeting and argue process first. If you're at the meeting discussing substantive matters and part of the group is discussing process, call time-out and get the group on the same track.

SEPARATE PROBLEMS FROM PEOPLE

Relationships among those at the meeting can be as important and determinative of outcome as the issue under discussion, particularly when relationships are ongoing. Abe will often be as concerned about how Bill reacts as he is about the proposal on the table. It is understandable that people want to maintain working relationships while discussing sometimes volatile issues.

However, as a result, relationships tend to become entangled in the issues under discussion. The problem has been well stated by Harvard Law School professors Roger Fisher and William Ury: "On both the giving and receiving end, we are likely to treat people and problems as one. Within the family, a statement such as 'The kitchen is a mess' or 'Our bank account is low' may be intended simply to identify a problem, but it is likely to be heard as a personal attack."

A colleague of mine used to say, far too often, "The facts speak for themselves." He was wrong; facts seldom speak for themselves. When you're dealing with people, the perception of facts is more important than the facts themselves. The truth, the "facts," are just other arguments heard in different ways, and they are often heard in different ways depending upon who has presented them.

Try to separate substantive problems from the people. You can do this by being conscious of the tendency for the two to be entangled, by addressing the perceptions as real instead of irrelevant, and by accepting emotions without reacting emotionally to them.

THE ORDER OF DISCUSSION

When confronting an issue, think about ordering discussion in the following way:

1. Seek agreement on the basic problem and the goal you want to achieve.

2. Gather the facts.

3. Separate problems when there are more than one.

4. Ask for a multiple of solutions.

5. Pick the best solution.

6. Decide who does what to implement the solution.

7. Make sure it gets done.

Author Anthony Jay has suggested a parallel approach for discussion that you might find easier to remember. It follows exactly the same pattern as a visit to the doctor:

1. *"What seems to be the problem?"* Something seems wrong; get it on the table.

2. *"How long has this been going on?"* This is gathering the facts, the case history of the illness.

3. *"Would you just lie down on the couch?"* A more detailed examination of facts, distinguishing particular problems from other problems.

4. *"You seem to have slipped a disk."* A diagnosis is offered. You should actually look for more than one.

5. *"Take this prescription to the druggist."* A solution to solve the problem. Here the doctor offers one solution, whereas any group should offer many solutions prior to deciding on one.

BEGINNING AT THE SAME PLACE

Before the group undertakes a discussion, identify where you are in the discussion process. Assume that your partners will start at a different point. Bring them together. Otherwise, your participants will be confused. For example, you believe your company's current ad agency is doing a poor job. You want to recommend to your boss two alternative companies, if you can find them. You want the help of two associates in picking the two companies. You call a meeting together, but the first words out of the mouth of one of your associates is, "I don't believe we need an ad agency if we ourselves would just focus on some other marketing techniques." Your peer is not yet prepared to focus on picking two alternative companies because he's not sure that any ad agency is the goal. Before he begins providing the best input he may have on the relative strengths of competing ad agencies, he has to be convinced (or told) that the task is to pick an agency, not to decide whether any agency should be picked. If he's a subordinate, you can just direct the goal, although you'll have more creativity and commitment if you persuade him. If he's a peer, you need a mandate to set the goal, or you're going to have to come to the goal together through discussion.

However, if your meeting partners have gathered momentum and are about to take action, be careful as a participant not to go back over old ground and begin the whole discussion again. "It just drives me nuts," says Foothill Group's Don Gevirtz, "when one of my staff wants to rehash a subject we've already left, when we're in the middle of acting on another. The time for him to have made his comment was earlier."

ALWAYS KNOW WHERE YOU ARE

As a check before and during the meeting, ask yourself what the purpose of a particular item of discussion is and what steps should have *preceded* it. If discussion seems disorganized, go back through the logical order of discussion presented earlier and make sure there is agreement on preceding steps. If necessary, go back and reconfirm agreement on earlier stages. Always make sure that the discussion has not turned prematurely toward doing a new task. And once a task is completed, ask what the next step is and who or what group is expected to undertake it.

Distinguishing process and substance and separating and ordering tasks are among the most critical techniques for ensuring a win rather than a loss at any meeting. The men and women who have mastered these techniques are invariably the top performers in their businesses or professions. They know *what* they want to achieve and *how* to achieve it. The means may be subtle or direct, persuasive or authoritarian, depending upon the individual's style and position—but the results are always the same.

Part Five

SPECIAL STRATEGIES FOR HANDLING SPECIAL SITUATIONS

No one is born a master.

—ITALIAN PROVERB

CHAPTER SIXTEEN

Tips for Leading the Meeting

THE CHAIRMAN SHOULD NOT ONLY BE FAMILIAR
WITH PARLIAMENTARY USAGE, AND SET THE EX-
AMPLE OF STRICT CONFORMITY THERETO, BUT HE
SHOULD BE A MAN OF EXECUTIVE ABILITY, CAPA-
BLE OF CONTROLLING MEN. HE SHOULD SET AN
EXAMPLE OF COURTESY, AND SHOULD NEVER FOR-
GET THAT TO CONTROL OTHERS, IT IS NECESSARY
TO CONTROL ONE'S SELF.

—From *Robert's Rules of Order*, 1876

YOU can very nearly predict the success of any meeting by who's chairing it. The chair is half the meeting, not because of what he or she can contribute substantively, but because a good chair is a prerequisite for controlling the meeting process.

The chair is more like a referee or coach than a quarterback, although at times he must be a little of all three. He is more the producer/director of the play than one of the actors, although at certain times he must be the star. And in other situations, whether dealing for himself or representing a particular side, he is the captain of a team looking for a win. From nearly any perspective, however, the chair must be a leader. And to be a leader, a meeting master, he should also see himself as a servant of the group.

CONTROL AND AUTHORITY

The authority of a superior over subordinates is not difficult to maintain. But how does the chair maintain discipline in a group of peers so that he can keep the meeting on track? In fact, among peers, authority and discipline come from the *chair's perceived commitment to the group and the group's objective*, as well as from his skill in assisting the group in meeting the objective. If the chair is perceived to have his own agenda, or if he is perceived to favor some group members over others, his authority will be limited to that which he can muster on a particular vote. If, however, the chair can embody a commitment to every member of the group and a common objective, his strength and authority go deeper. In maintaining order and discipline, he will be seen as imposing not *his* will upon the individual who may be endangering the process, but rather the group's will. As such, his voice will represent many others, and his authority will be greater.

For the chair, then, more than anyone else at the meeting, Mies van der Rohe's statement is true: Less is more. His comments as well as his goals should be limited. The less he says about particulars, the greater his strength. His primary concerns should be the welfare of the group, the integrity of the meeting process, the achievement of the group objective, and the aim and objectives of the company or institution as a whole. The less he imposes his views on particular matters, the more able he is to serve these higher goals.

QUALITIES OF THE CHAIR

"Chairing a meeting, like leadership in general, is as much an art as it is a science," says Arista Records President Clive Davis. "Still, one can always perfect one's art." In chairing any meeting, you should attempt to develop and apply a variety of qualities.

VISION

This is the ability to imagine the meeting in your head before it ever takes place and the ability to align the meeting with the fundamental goals of the group, the cause, or the organization. Management expert Peter Drucker says, "Effective executives know what they expect to get out of a meeting.... They insist that the meeting serve the contribution [or cause] to which they have committed themselves."

Without this vision, including an almost intuitive understanding of the strategic goal, the specific purpose of the meeting, the measurable objectives sought to be achieved, and the steps to be taken to achieve them, you will be lost in the chaos that naturally confronts every meeting. Norman Lear phrases it this way: The chair is "someone who understands the spine of the meeting and sees his way through the minutiae and unrelated events so as to adhere to that spine."

Such a vision need not *originate* with you. In fact, in

many meetings the vision originates with a staff person or another member who may not have direct responsibility for running the meeting. But you must be able to grasp the vision and apply it during the meeting, whether you have developed it yourself or have come to understand it through others.

Just as important as this vision is the ability to *share it* with your meeting partners. By sharing the vision, you can bring the group mind into focus and cooperation so that it can more effectively police itself during the meeting and achieve the desired goal.

PEOPLE SKILLS

Managing a meeting is managing people. Those with poor "people skills" seldom make successful chairs. We are not talking here of the individual with the nice personality. It is the person who has developed the skills to motivate and lead in a positive way, to be able to listen and hear what meeting partners are saying, to sense when there is confusion or harmony, discord or agreement, and to be able to bring people and ideas together in a constructive way.

WISDOM

Closely allied with people skills is what, in discussing the general qualities of leadership, Warren Bennis and Burt Nanus in their book *Leaders* have called "emotional wisdom," including the following skills:

1. The ability to accept people as they are, not as you would like them to be.

232

2. The capacity to approach people, relationships, and problems in terms of the present rather than the past.

3. The ability to treat those you are close to with the same courteous attention you extend to strangers and casual acquaintances.

4. The ability to trust others even if the risk is great.

5. The ability to do without constant approval and recognition from others.

FLEXIBILITY

Adhering to the spine of the meeting does not mean a militaristic devotion to the agenda or the time if it appears that a deviation can more clearly focus the contributions of meeting members toward the desired goal. "The [effective chair] goes into his meeting with an agenda," says Harold Geneen, former chairman of the board of ITT, "but to him the timetable is not nearly as important as what might arise unexpectedly at the meeting. The most important item of the day could turn up at the end of the time allotted to that subject.... Of course digressions, repetitions, and pontifications should be squelched unmercifully. He can and should keep control over the meeting, moving it right along. But he should know, too, when not to cut off discussion."

How do you know? Only by first envisioning the goal and the contribution the meeting can make toward achieving it, and then *listening* very carefully.

DECIDE YOUR POSITION BEFORE THE MEETING

You should, if possible, decide *tentatively* all major issues prior to the meeting you will chair. You should remain flexible; you should be prepared to change your mind. But you should make the effort to form preliminary opinions on all issues prior to the meeting. In fact, you should do so largely before you call the meeting.

You must do this for at least two reasons. First, you are, after all, an important person to the meeting, and your opinions and judgments are equally important and may even be decisive. But during the meeting you should remain neutral. If you indicate your position, you will not get input from subordinates. If you argue your position with peers, you will have difficulty paying attention to the process and put your own identity over the integrity of the group. Your attention *must* be directed almost entirely to the process of meeting, not to its substance. Therefore, your time for substantive involvement during the meeting is limited, and you must make up for that by focusing more on the substance before the meeting.

Second, you must try to predict which issues require more or less discussion and debate in order to structure the meeting effectively. You may conclude that some items need further study before coming before the group, or that some items can be approved almost by consent. You ought to decide whether certain matters are even worthy of a meeting. Of course,

234

you must be prepared to change your mind, but you will lose perspective and control unless you force yourself to make a prejudgment, however tentative.

How and When You Can Influence the Substance

What gets on the agenda is usually more important than anything said, so you wield great power when you set the agenda. If you want to influence substance in the meeting, it should be done subtly and sparingly. Once you have determined which issues, if any, are particularly important to you (or the organization), you should determine whether there is likely to be any disagreement. Generally, where there is none, you should have no interest in involving yourself in discussion. Nor should you have interest (as chair) where there is overwhelming opposition to your position on an issue.

Only on issues of highest priority affecting fundamental matters, where your action can alter the outcome, should you marshal your energies to influence decisions. Depending upon your goal, your first method should be to see to what extent you can narrow the issue or get it decided in your favor prior to the meeting, so as to avoid using your authority when chair. Next—but only in matters of highest concern—you must see if you can influence the outcome by procedural means without voicing an opinion. Only when all other efforts fail should you attempt to influence the outcome by expressing substantive opinions. In general, if you want a particular point to be advocated strongly at the meeting, you should enlist another member to make that point. You will be more effective supporting someone else's point than making your own.

In the end, your continuing effectiveness as chair—a strong, neutral, and fair party, the embodiment of the *whole* group—is more important than your effectiveness on any one issue. You should not sacrifice the former for the latter. The most important issues, and the ones for which you must certainly take the risks, are those that impact upon the basic authority, integrity, and effectiveness of the group and its cause.

COMMUNICATING

One of the most important functions performed by you as chair is to facilitate communication. You must facilitate communication among the individual members of the group, *and* you must be the principal voice of the "group mind." Therefore you must be constantly on the lookout for possible miscommunications. It is not enough that you simply note their occurrence. You must do what you can to prevent and correct miscommunications. Watch out for the following common communication problems:

1. The tendency of members to use words whose meanings are unclear or ambiguous.

2. The tendency to generalize to such an extent that any meaning in the particular case is lost.

3. The tendency of each member to presume that other members are thinking what he is thinking.

4. The tendency of the group or its members to miss the context in which a statement is made.

5. The tendency of the group to stampede and take the last statement as the final statement.

A CHECKLIST FOR THE CHAIR

Although it may seem that some people take to chairing a meeting like a duck to water, that ability is usually the result of hard work and long experience. If you bear in mind the following fundamental principles, some of which have been discussed earlier, you will be well on your way to success in chairing almost any meeting.

1. *Envision what's going to happen.* Script the meeting in advance on paper or in your head. You may not know the outcome of all issues or the points that may illuminate or distract. There will be original thoughts and new information. But get a sense for the "spine" of the meeting and understand where the meeting should go. Your preparation should tell you as much as possible about where the problems are. You, of all participants, must begin with a conception of what you want to have accomplished when the meeting is over. Then choose a "theater" that will work toward your goals.

2. *Limit the participants.* If you can, reduce the number of people actively participating to those necessary to effect the goal. If the composition is set, review the participants with an eye toward their abilities, personalities, and leadership skills.

3. *Define your role in relation to your meeting partners.* Are you a peer, a subordinate, or the superior? Once defined, determine how you will facilitate the special requirements of your role. As a peer, do you have a mandate? As a superior, how can you make your subordinates feel comfortable? As a subordinate, will you have a mandate for action when the meeting is over?

4. *Limit issues.* If you can, limit issues to those that are required or necessary. Prioritize the issues to be discussed.

5. *Prepare a working agenda.* Then get it "blessed" by key participants, particularly if they are peers, and share it with all participants.

6. *Arrive early.* Unless you're in an exalted position of authority that almost demands that you arrive later (few of us will ever be in such positions), arrive early and get a feel for the room and the situation. Look for problems with the seating, lighting, or anything else that may add to or detract from the meeting. If you can, mingle with some of the early arrivers. Look for personal attitudes and agendas. Also, look to establish rapport with individual participants; these are "meetings within meetings" that can have their own objectives but can also serve the overall objectives of the meeting.

7. *Unite with the group.* You are automatically set apart from the group because you are the chair. The distance is a blessing because of the authority it gives you. But it can also engender resentment, both conscious and subconscious. In order to function effectively, you need to break down barriers between you and the group. Smile, be friendly, offer compliments. Join in side discussions before the meeting and at breaks. As the meeting progresses, focus on uniting the group members rather than dividing them.

Encourage participants to focus on the facts rather than on personalities.

8. *Start on time.* There is more to starting on time than simply getting through earlier. Starting on time is the first test of your control. It sets a subconscious expectation with respect to your ability to perform throughout the meeting. If you can't do the first thing you said you were going to do, why should your leadership be taken seriously? It also establishes a presumption that the meeting as a whole will be a success. It establishes the ground rules for others who are presenting, reporting, or discussing issues. There will always be the tendency to put off starting the meeting until a few latecomers arrive. Don't succumb. When you begin starting on time, you'll be surprised at how quickly people arrive on time.

9. *Beginning the meeting.* "He who has made a good beginning has half the deed done," said Cicero. The beginning sets the stage for the remainder of the meeting. There should be no doubt that the meeting has begun, no weak start. Bang the gavel or speak louder than you have to; do whatever you can theatrically to make it clear that you've begun. Where appropriate, try increasing the volume and seriousness of your voice to denote the beginning of the enterprise. Whether you're chairing the board or making a presentation to supervisors, never begin with an apology. You will only program failure. Rather, show confidence and strength. That does not mean you ought to leave humor out; it can be a very effective weapon. What you should be attempting in the beginning is to distinguish the feeling immediately prior to the meeting from the feeling once the meeting has begun: "This is business."

10. *Get any announcements out of the way early and as quickly as possible.* These are information items that can

often be distributed on paper before the meeting. When that isn't possible, you must still remember that these are not items for discussion; don't allow an information item to be turned into an item for debate.

11. *State the purpose, objectives, and estimated time for the meeting.* This is your most important statement at the meeting. If you fail here, the meeting will start off track. You must inform (or remind) the group of the objective the meeting seeks to achieve. This is your opportunity to focus the group mind and give the members the goal to shoot for. State the objective and process clearly. By stating time limits, you will give everyone an instinctive sense of the pacing required to get the job done.

12. *If someone comes in late.* Neither draw attention to such a person by restating what has preceded nor admonish the member for his or her tardiness. In either case you are only adding a further distraction. If it's a constant problem, say something after the meeting, such as "It would help me a great deal if you could try to get here on time. The others follow your example and are starting to show up late as well." If you know in advance someone will be arriving late or leaving early, note it for the group so it does not appear to be a criticism of you or the meeting.

13. *Restate the objective periodically.* Presume there is unspoken confusion or drift and periodically remind the group why they're there and what it is that's being sought at a given moment.

14. *Represent the group to the group.* The eyes of meeting partners tend to fix on the chair. Therefore, what the chair says, how she looks, how he sits, become the mirror for the group in assessing itself. Be careful at all times to reflect what you believe the group should think of itself.

Ninety percent of what you say should be reflective of the group or the process rather than of you as an individual.

15. *Remain impartial or at least demonstrate an appearance of impartiality.* You cannot maintain your credibility if you are involved in the debate of issues, nor can you function effectively to get the best out of every member and keep the meeting on track. Limit your statements to a single short sentence whenever you speak; your focus is process, and what you have to say about process can almost always be said in a single sentence.

16. *Separate fact from beliefs and opinions.* Whenever you can, distinguish between facts and information that the group may record as fact. You don't want to get into arguments with members, but be careful that the group mind does not record as facts points you know to be matters of opinion or simply untrue.

17. *Watch the pacing.* Keep an eye on the time and the feelings of the group. Look for opportunities to take breaks if necessary. Be concerned and show concern about the group's comfort.

18. *Be on the lookout for emotional buildups.* If you see signs of anger or frustration, attempt to mollify them early on.

19. *Seek contributions.* Don't force anyone to speak, but make sure that the more reticent members have the opportunity. Ask them, from time to time, whether they have something to add on a particular point. Actively look for disagreement so that it can be dealt with.

20. *Make people feel important.* Find what is positive about a contribution from any member of the group, rather than what's negative. Look for opportunities to make

241

members feel good about themselves and their contributions. Record their contributions; it's a sign of respect. Be generous with compliments.

21. *Clarify.* Summarize points of agreement and clarify opposing points of view. People hear things differently. Your job is to make sure that each person is recording information the same way.

22. *Take it step by step.* When a particular issue or task is completed, state the conclusion and make sure everyone is together before you go on to the next phase or issue. Make clear what has been completed and what has been left open.

23. *Protect the weak.* Make sure that minority views are expressed. Look out for the stampede that generally follows presentation of an idea. Many people want to jump on the bandwagon by either knocking the idea or praising it. They want action. Ask those in favor to express potential problems; ask those opposed whether they can't see the good. Look out for the little guy.

24. *Divide problems.* Divide big problems into subproblems and address them separately wherever possible.

25. *Keep the meeting moving.* Don't permit long time pauses. Attempt to feel when the issue is ripe for conclusion and offer your summary. Attempt to give the meeting a sense of momentum and continuing success.

26. *Ending the meeting.* Summarize what has been accomplished and relate the conclusions to the original intent of the meeting as stated in your agenda and opening statement. Go over what the next steps are. End in a positive, upbeat fashion. Make the members feel the meeting was worth their time and effort. The end of the meeting should be as clear as the beginning. Try to end on time.

WHEN THE CHAIR MUST DELIVER BAD NEWS

There comes a time in your life when you must deliver bad news. It may be firing an employee. It may be announcing the closure of a division. It may be a death in the company. On these occasions, the chair—the leader—embodies the institution. Be courteous, concerned, and as gracious as possible, but you do no one a service by dragging out the task, by hinting at meaning instead of confronting the issue directly. A CEO I once knew had a meeting to terminate an employee. The employee had been in his office about twenty minutes when suddenly the door was flung open and she ran out screaming, "Square pegs, round holes—I don't know what you're talking about! I'm a human being." The office buzzed for a week.

"I tell my employees," says former Shaklee Chairman Gary Shansby, "if you have to deliver bad news to a group of people, put both feet squarely on the ground, put your hands together in front of you, look them straight in the eyes, and deliver the message. Then be around later to answer individual concerns."

SELECTING THE CHAIR

For all those who think that they would make an excellent chair, there are others for whom the very idea of leading a group is frightening. With time and experience that fear can be overcome. But the truth is that not everyone has the ability or skills to be an effective chair. So with so much riding on it, why is it that so many groups or organizations, when they have the opportunity, choose to pass the chairmanship around as if the post were the equivalent of blackboard monitor in the third grade?

"Let's give more people a chance to chair," some say. Or, "Shouldn't we be democratic and give everyone a turn?" Absolutely not! Not unless the meeting means very little to you. Remember, you are winning and losing in every meeting you attend. You are either getting somewhere or nowhere, for you, for your cause, or for your organization. Don't jeopardize all this by picking a weak chair out of kindness. You help no one.

When you have a choice (and often you don't), selecting a chair will be the *most important decision you make*. If you make that choice on any basis other than "who's the best for the job," you will be compromising everything else you do and every moment you spend in connection with the meeting or meetings. It's like rotating the quarterback's job among the other persons playing on the team. Once you've made a wrong choice, you cannot make up for it by manipulating the chairperson during the meeting. Correcting him, challenging him, questioning him will only undermine the meeting further. You've got to bite the bullet in the selection.

Now, as a superior, you may choose to give the opportunity to chair meetings to your team members from time to time. That's different. It provides room for growth and can free you to contribute to the substance of the meetings you attend more often. Sharing leadership in this way is healthy. But otherwise, pick the person to serve as chair who most clearly embodies the abilities and skills required to do the best job. "The question 'Who ought to be the boss?' is like asking 'Who ought to be the tenor in the quartet?'" said Henry Ford. "Obviously, the man who can sing tenor."

In selecting a chair, if you believe yourself to be the best person for the job, you will still have to prove it by displaying all of the skills and abilities that make for effective meetings. If you believe that someone can handle the job better, it may be to your long-term advantage to select that person. But at the same time, you should take every opportunity to sharpen your own leadership skills. The ability to lead, to get things done, is the most important ingredient in career success. And if you can gain the ability to lead effective meetings, so much the better for you and your career.

CHAPTER SEVENTEEN
Making the Most of Brief Encounters

LET US THEN BE UP AND DOING.

—Henry Wadsworth Longfellow

OUR information society's "quick bite" meeting, and a healthy one, too, is the "brief encounter." These are the unscheduled ad hoc meetings, usually with no more than four people and preferably only two. Brief encounters, including phone calls, are critical to good management and communication because they tend to (1) limit attention to a specific issue; (2) avoid the "fat" of the scheduled meeting; and (3) provide a way to limit scheduled meetings. By its nature, the brief encounter reduces the tasks attempted to be performed, reduces the number of people actively participating, reduces the time spent, minimizes the impact of the meeting environment, and minimizes the likelihood of a loss of control in general. In other words, the brief encounter tends to be a pretty good meeting in some important ways. But "tends to be" and "is" are two different things. A lack of some strategic thought and preparation will doom a brief encounter just as

246

easily as any meeting. Because they are brief, we tend to wing it. But, in fact, the luxury of less time in meeting demands a serious, clear focus and solid preparation, even when the time for preparation is short.

AVOIDING THE FAT OF THE SCHEDULED MEETING

The scheduled meeting necessarily contains some fat: introductions, courtesies, theater, and the repetition expected and required when a group of people attempt to complete a task together. A certain amount of fat in scheduled meetings is as important to a good meeting as a certain amount of fat is to a good piece of beef. You cannot and should not eliminate it entirely.

But the expectations and requirements of a brief encounter are different; it is the lean cuisine of meetings. You walk down the hall, put your head in the boss's office, and say, "Have you got a minute?" If he does, you're on. Or you pick up the phone to call a client or customer. In each case, you are expected to get to the issue immediately: the issues are limited, the participants have been defined, the time is short.

The brief encounter is frightening for some employers and some employees: those who make a career of meetings but avoid the meat of any meeting. The brief encounter is all beef. Thus, many employers will go out of their way to create a scheduled meeting with more participants when the brief encounter is actually the better meeting tool. When you are attempting to reduce your meetings and limit participants, your best alternative may be the brief encounter.

PREPARING FOR BRIEF ENCOUNTERS

Preparation time for a brief encounter may be somewhat shorter, but the questions are always the same.

1. What do you want to have accomplished when the
   brief encounter is over?

2. What type of task is being attempted (sharing information, delegating, deciding, brainstorming)?

3. By what yardstick will you distinguish success from
   failure?

4. What's your relation to your meeting partner, and
   what type of participation do you want to elicit (superior, peer, or subordinate)?

5. Is there anything that must occur prior to the meeting to make it effective?

6. Finally, visualize this short, prospective meeting in
   your head as you would like it to take place. Then
   go for it.

FOLLOW-UP

Follow-up is even more important for a brief encounter than it is for larger, regularly scheduled meetings. You do not have the group to provide additional
pressure to complete tasks. Probably some who are affected by decisions reached or actions taken were not

at the meeting. And because it was not scheduled, it will be less likely to appear on someone's follow-up list. That's why it's important to take notes after a brief encounter if something of substance has been decided. Clearly state what that decision was and who is expected to do what. Follow up with a short memo to those affected, whether or not they attended.

CONVERTING SCHEDULED MEETINGS TO BRIEF ENCOUNTERS

Try to convert scheduled meetings to brief encounters whenever you can. It's a good way to say no to meetings; it's a good way to be more efficient. It's also a good way to weed out unnecessary participants. When someone says, "I'd like to get together for lunch to talk about 'X,'" ask yourself whether it can be handled in a brief encounter "right now." If the answer is yes, you'll find that you have saved time arranging the lunch (in addition to the hour or so for lunch itself), which you could use in a more productive way with somebody else or alone.

Brief encounters, or meetings within meetings, may also occur immediately prior to larger meetings. Do not, however, interrupt meetings in process for brief encounters. You only undermine the meeting. When someone wants to talk individual business during a meeting with others, simply say that you and he should discuss the matter immediately *after* the meeting.

249

BEFORE YOU PICK UP THE TELEPHONE

You can avoid many wasted meetings simply by handling them by phone. When you can't, you can't. But you should try. In any event, keep in mind that a phone call is a contemporary substitute for a meeting or letter. Be as prepared, as thoughtful, and as courteous in your phone calls as in your meetings. Before you pick up the phone to make a call, ask:

1. What do I want to have accomplished when this phone call is over?

2. What task (brainstorming, information exchange, decision making) is being performed?

3. How do I distinguish success from failure?

4. What's my relation to my phone partner?

5. What, if anything, must be completed prior to the phone call to meet my objective?

Again, visualize the phone conversation, make necessary notes, and devise a plan for following up.

SAVING TIME

Research by A.T.&T. shows that fewer than one in four business calls reach the right person at a time when it's convenient to talk. That's a great deal of wasted time and effort. The solution? Don't accept telephone tag as the natural order. Telephone management consultant George Walther suggests that you reach further with each call, try harder. If you can't get through to the person you want to talk to, leave a detailed message as to what you want to cover. Ask when your contact will be available and schedule the call. Don't be satisfied simply because you made the call if you really want to save time and accomplish something.

PHONE IMPRESSIONS

When you meet in person, you communicate—sometimes unintentionally—with your appearance, your timeliness, your style, your body language. When you meet by phone, everything depends on your voice. If your voice is weak, you appear weak. If your words are vague, you will seem indecisive. If your phrasing is negatively worded, you will give an impression of lack of confidence. Speak clearly and firmly, and use positively constructed sentences. For example, instead of saying, "I can't get you the letter until Friday," say, "I'll get you the letter on Friday."

You should also be sensitive to the impression made by the person who answers your phone or places your call. That person represents you and your organization to anybody on the other end of the line. Their "introduction" sets you up to appear competent or incompetent, organized or disorganized. Make sure the impression is the one you want since it may be all someone on the other end knows about you or your organization. Since you may not be aware of the impression your office creates, try making "cold calls" to your office from time to time to see how incoming calls are handled.

CONFERENCE CALLS

Conference calls may be the most difficult form of meeting because of the potential for confusion. As a general rule, avoid conference calls unless you are only looking for ideas or you are asking for acquiescence to a predetermined decision. Information can be just as quickly shared by telex or telecopier or even overnight mail. When you do meet by conference call, you should have all pertinent information, including a detailed agenda, in the hands of your phone partners prior to the meeting. As chair, you're going to have to work harder to avoid miscommunication. As a participant, strictly limit comments to the specific point under discussion. It is a good idea for each speaker to identify himself each time he speaks. The chair should summarize clearly and follow with a written report of the action taken.

COURTESY

When making a phone call, remember that you are busy and the person on the other end of the line is busy. Your tendency will be to be abrupt, which may force you to deliver a "message"—by your tone of voice—that you don't intend. At the same time, it may take a moment to get the other guy's attention, for he will no doubt be doing something else when you reach him. Therefore, in all telephone meetings, give extra care to courtesy.

UNINTENDED BRIEF ENCOUNTERS

You're at your table in a restaurant, waiting for your luncheon companion, when a business associate says hello. You may ask him to sit for a moment, or you might not. In either case, a brief encounter ensues. For some people these "meetings" are nuisances. For the meeting master, they are always opportunities. Instead of deflecting a conversation, ask yourself what you could possibly accomplish with this person in this limited exchange. Your goal may be simply to be friendly, to remain on good terms. In that case, showing courtesy and enthusiasm may be your task. But perhaps there is some piece of information you could elicit or some favor you could request. Perhaps you could delegate or share work on a project of mutual interest. Think, even if it's for only a moment. What is your role in relation to him? What does he expect? This person will walk away with an impression of you on the basis of this exchange that may be stronger than one formed in a planned meeting of ten people. Or you may be able to accomplish something that would otherwise take more time. In this unintended brief encounter, your goals must be severely limited, but your impact can be huge because nothing else is on the table. So when you find yourself in an unintended brief encounter, give your attention to your partner, but quickly assess in the back of your mind what you want to have accomplished when the encounter is over.

KEEPING COMMUNICATION OPEN

Brief encounters are especially valuable for establishing and maintaining communication. The larger the group, the more difficult real communication is. Try to utilize brief encounters between regularly scheduled meetings in order to assure follow-up, to seek or offer advice in confidence, to motivate, and to keep communication lines open. Look for opportunities to share something of yourself. Brief encounters are just that— brief. But that does not mean the goal is *only* business. Maintaining good communication may at some point be far more important than any substantive issue. You can't often address particular interpersonal matters in large groups. Use brief encounters to focus on individuals.

COMMON ABUSES OF BRIEF ENCOUNTERS

The most common abuse of the brief encounter is failure to focus on the goal. But be watchful of these other common problems:

1. The tendency to decide on the spot things that require further consultation with a larger group or further thought and analysis. Brief encounters offer participants the opportunity to divide and conquer: to approach individuals independently and seek approval for actions or policies that are more appropriately addressed by a group as a whole. For someone seeking to obtain a particular decision, brief encounters are a strategic tool. As a superior or a peer who must make a decision, be careful that you do not make pre-

cipitous choices without necessary consultation with others.

2. The tendency to turn brief encounters into idle chatter continuing for a length of time in no way related to the goal. If the purpose is to maintain friendly relations, some idle conversation is necessary. But make certain the parties are not simply seeking to avoid problems or other work.

3. The tendency to give less than full attention. When you've asked someone to join you in your office, don't continue shuffling papers, don't continually pick up the phone, and don't assume you can handle the brief encounter while focusing part of your attention on something else.

In general, try to use brief encounters more and scheduled meetings less. Particularly when the agenda is short—a single issue or two—scheduled meetings only become clubs looking for problems. But when you find that more than two or three people are required, it is wise to turn to the scheduled meeting, including the goal setting, preparation, and theater necessary to make it effective.

CHAPTER EIGHTEEN

Combat: Winning
Your Point of View

DO NOT GET INTO A FIGHT IF YOU CAN POSSIBLY
AVOID IT. IF YOU GET IN IT, SEE IT THROUGH.
DON'T HIT IF IT IS HONORABLY POSSIBLE TO
AVOID HITTING, BUT NEVER HIT SOFT. DON'T HIT
AT ALL IF YOU CAN HELP IT; DON'T HIT A MAN IF
YOU CAN POSSIBLY AVOID IT; BUT IF YOU DO HIT
HIM, PUT HIM TO SLEEP.

—Theodore Roosevelt

THE purpose of most meetings is not to win an argument but to act collectively, through clear and honest communication, to achieve a common goal. However, there *are* meetings in which you want your point of view to prevail. *Be careful.* It's all too easy to get your ego caught up in arguments and forget the real goal. Only you can weigh the importance of a particular point of view against your overall relations with meeting partners, your individual goals, and the goals you should have in common. But even the meeting masters do battle on occasion.

PREPARATIONS FOR BATTLE

It has often been said that most battles are won or lost before they are ever fought. And, like everything else about meetings, most points are substantially won or lost before the meeting begins. Thus, if you are in for a fight, you must give careful consideration to and, if possible, gain control of the meeting composition, the theater, and the agenda. If you have to wait for the meeting to take place to know whether you've got the "votes" to carry your point, you're very much at risk. The amateur walks in thinking he's so smart and glib that his oratory will win the day. The meeting master knows that any meeting can self-destruct. He may not get the opportunity to respond at the right time; others may make better arguments; deals may have already been cut. The meeting master prepares thoroughly for a win.

PERSONAL RECONNAISSANCE

Before he puts himself in a position where he could lose publicly (and thereby demonstrate weakness), the meeting master wants to know the odds of winning and the risks to him and other meeting members. He knows that his meeting partners will also want to weigh risks of battle. That requires some personal reconnaissance before the meeting. You can learn what your partners' problems are. You can learn the strength and weaknesses of your case and that of your opponents *as your meeting partners view it* (the most important view). You can learn what additional work must be done to turn people around. You can learn these things without putting yourself in a corner with other members holding different views. There are many reasons people might vote with you or against you. And in all-out battle, you want a vote, for whatever reason may justify it. To be effective, you've got to know who's influenced by what, and by the time of the meeting it's probably too late.

THE CHAIR

The person whose preliminary views are most important to know is the chair. As we've seen, he can control the outcome of a meeting in a variety of ways. He does not have to be for you, but it's hard work if he's against you. Try to move the chair as far as you can in your direction before the meeting, whether that means on process or substance. Be sympathetic to his role as neutral leader. It may be more important to you where he places the item on the agenda than that he votes your way.

THE TRIAL BALLOON

In general, when you're presenting a new idea, don't wait until the meeting to test it. Offer a trial balloon to a few people far enough in advance of the meeting to be able to work out any problems. Look at the trial balloon as an opportunity to get others to take a personal interest in your idea. You'll not only improve the idea, you'll gather votes.

ADVANCED WARNINGS

Your personal reconnaissance should give you some advanced warning of potential problems, but you should also seek to give advance warnings to allies when you see problems ahead for them. In addition, if you're planning to take some action at the meeting that may negatively impact on someone else, consider giving some warning on this, too. If there's justification for your position, a fellow participant may be understanding; if you fail to give notice, you've made a greater enemy.

GET TO THE MEETING EARLY

Sometimes a great deal is accomplished in the few minutes before a meeting begins: people show their cards, deals are cut. You will want to be aware of this premeeting maneuvering. Also, seek to get a feel for the general attitude of your partners. Are they in a feisty mood? Is there room for compromise? Are people pressed for time? Does a particular issue seem to cause common concern? Try to be a part of the group as quickly as possible.

OTHER PREMEETING DECISIONS

Think through all the points involved in handling the meeting at which you will fight for your idea: location, timing, composition, theater, relationships. Some may be within your control, some may be outside your control; some may bear upon your battle, some may not. Try to influence any that you believe can affect the outcome of your battle.

AT THE MEETING

STYLE

In general, don't change your basic style when you're attempting to win an argument; it's the surest giveaway that something's wrong with your message. If you have employed combat techniques sparingly in the past, you've probably built a reputation for honesty and fairness. On this occasion you can utilize that reputation, but not if you *look* as if you've left these qualities behind. Within your general style you may want to raise the decibel level of your voice or argue the case more emphatically, but be careful that your *motives* do not appear to have changed—that is, you're still that same honest, fair, and decent person looking to benefit the whole group.

DON'T WASTE YOUR BULLETS

Don't get mixed up in other issues unless you can see how your involvement helps win converts to your point of view on the issue you want to win. Meeting partners can be easily offended when you disagree with them. If winning your point is that important to you, don't offend your potential votes by arguing about issues that are not meaningful to you. Also, for many meeting partners there is an implicit if mis-placed sense of fairness about spreading the "wins" around. You may hear something like "Well, Pete got his way on the budget issue, so I thought it was only fair that Sandy have her way on the new project." By the time your issue comes up, you want to be perceived as being owed a vote, not owing a vote. If necessary, reach agreement with others on issues of particular concern to them in order to have them favorably disposed to you on your issue.

CONTRIBUTE EARLY

When the issue is one you care about, contribute early. Research has indicated that when a person contributes early in the discussion, he is more likely to exert greater influence throughout the discussion. You want to indicate where you stand so that others with mildly opposing views are less inclined to get into the act. Often a stampede will develop around a viewpoint. You don't want that stampede to be an opposing view; it's too much work to turn it around. Likewise, be prepared to come back into the discussion to combat opposing points. These two techniques—contributing early and contributing to combat opposing points—go hand in hand. You define the debate by your early contribution and force opponents to respond to you. Then you rebut their counterarguments. If you wait to contribute, the issue will be defined by your opponents, and you will be the one on the defensive. If you fail to contribute later, a skillful opponent may be able to take the offensive and redefine the debate.

MAKE YOUR POINT

Don't get lost in philosophy or preliminary statements; you will lose your meeting partners. Not all of them will follow you even when you're clear and simple. When you go off on tangents, that may be the only thing they hear. Before you speak, ask yourself what it is you want your meeting partners to remember—in one short sentence. Make sure you make that point first, then offer your supporting arguments, then repeat your point.

PROVIDE A WAY OUT

If you're disagreeing with someone, win or lose, try to provide your opponent a way out, a way to save face. Remember, your goal is to win your point, not to embarrass the other guy. What goes around comes around. Go out of your way not to make the other guy look foolish. If you disagree, first state what you agree about before noting where you disagree; support his position as modified by your own. Sometimes you can make tough criticism appear less personal by claiming that you're simply acting as "the devil's advocate," taking an extreme opposing view merely for the purpose of testing an idea that you believe has merit.

KNOW WHEN TO QUIT

If you've tallied the votes before the meeting and know your position is a winning one, don't waste your energy, your partners' time, and your chits arguing for your point of view. You will only offend the losers when there is nothing more to gain. Likewise, once you see you've got your point won, don't risk losing it by letting the issue drag on. In the words of Benjamin Disraeli, "Next to knowing when to seize an opportunity, the most important thing in life is to know when to forgo an advantage." Many people risk losing a point they've already won by permitting discussion to continue.

SPECIAL WEAPONS

Assuming you have the facts and the talent to make a winning argument, you need not go further. But if your case is weak, or if you've got a savvy opponent who may manipulate the group, consider any of these techniques:

1. *Seating:* Find the power spots; isolate your opponents and put yourself in a position of control.

2. *Guilt by association:* Associate the opposing idea or your opponent with a word or a fact that conjures in the minds of your meeting partners an "emotional filter." For instance, "That's like selling arms for hostages." Or remind your meeting partners of other negative notions with which your opponent or his proposal can be associated.

3. *Glittering generalities:* This is the opposite of guilt by association. Associate positive words and concepts with your own position. Or tie it to a policy that has proved successful before: "This is the same position we took on the Manchester Project, and we made millions."

4. *Transference:* To buttress your point, make reference to well-known and respected authorities, such as important books, reports, or the minutes of a previous meeting. "As Peters says in *In Search of Excellence...*"

5. *Testimonial:* Use the transference technique by referring to respected personalities, such as the head of your company. "Mr. Pinkerton always says guarantees are a waste of time, and this is a good example why."

6. *"We're all in this together":* Relate yourself and your position to your meeting partners, sharing other points that you have in common and mentioning successes you have had in the past. "Remember the old boilerplate deal we did together? This is just the same."

7. *Card stacking:* Cite only the strong points of your position and the arguments against you that can be easily dismissed. Don't make the other guy's case unless you can destroy it.

8. *Bandwagon:* Point out, if you can do so plausibly, that most people are already in favor of your position. The implication is your meeting partner must be wrong if he disagrees.

9. *Use props:* Props such as charts and graphs can divert attention from the substance of your proposal. If the substance of your proposal is weak, a first-class presentation will divert attention. The group will subconsciously vote on the presentation rather than the substance.

CHAOS AND OPPORTUNITY

Entrepreneur Michael Kassan had a problem. He and his partner had obtained the franchise for a fast-food chicken restaurant, El Pollo Loco, in Las Vegas, but his partner had negotiated a deal for development of the real estate that left almost nothing for them. Since the restaurant was what would make the building and land valuable, Kassan saw no reason why he and his partner should not participate in the land and building, too. A basic deal had been struck, but it was not yet in writing. When Kassan received the written documents, they contained additional unfavorable points that had not been negotiated. Kassan saw an opportunity. He attended the next meeting with the developers and figuratively tore the documents apart, calling the entire agreement overreaching. Chaos ensued as multiple understandings of what had previously occurred were discussed. Kassan seized his opportunity. "Look," he said, "I want to be in business with you. Let's not try to retrace who said this and who said that. Let's start over with a clean slate." And they did.

When chaos exists, opportunities exist. Because egos, feelings, and personal needs are almost always as important as logic, confusion changes the game board more than logic dictates. An insult is confused with an issue and can sometimes be traded for one. When you're losing, look for opportunities to create chaos or change the momentum by calling for a break or a postponement.

STRIKE WHEN THE IRON IS HOT

When chaos ensues, the group subconsciously appreciates a new agenda and plan. If you've got a plan, you can capture control of the meeting. Your plan should *appear* to offer something for all sides. It's got to give the group a way out. Sometimes the solution is simply a recess, and sometimes it's a whole compromise. In essence, you are momentarily stealing the chair. Don't overreach. Don't try to take it all. Bend the rules just enough to acquire an advantage or remove the advantage your opponents may have.

You cannot afford to wage big battles very often. If you're fighting a lot in your meetings, you're probably failing elsewhere. But when you do go to war, fight to win. You will establish a precedent that in future meetings will encourage others to yield rather than fight again.

CHAPTER NINETEEN
Techniques for Meeting Follow-Up

BY PERSEVERANCE THE SNAIL REACHED THE ARK.

—Caroline H. Spurgeon

No meeting is an end in itself. It is always intended for a greater purpose. Therefore, it's not really over when the meeting is over. Nearly any victory can be subverted and any loss forestalled by actions that take place *after* the meeting.

BASIC FOLLOW-UP

The meeting master focuses carefully on follow-through. It reflects an understanding of and a commitment to the objective of the meeting rather than merely the means toward that objective. He protects decisions in his favor and redefines issues he's lost. He manages through follow-up, and he judges the sophistication of his meeting partners by their own follow-up.

Make note of decisions reached and actions taken at

267

any meeting you attend. If you've been the leader, follow up with a memo to meeting partners summarizing actions taken and tasks delegated. And don't forget the "meetings within meetings"—the separate encounters with your meeting partners. If you were able to advance your cause or position through some exchange, follow up with a note immediately after the meeting, taking the encounter a step further toward your goal. If you've been given an assignment as part of a meeting, do it quickly. Just as important, let the appropriate persons know it's been done.

SHARING RESULTS

Everyone who has briefed United States Senator Edward Kennedy in connection with a foreign trip gets at minimum a written summary and more often a phone call or personal meeting with the senator, briefing *them* on what took place in his meetings relative to *their* area of interest and expertise. He does this for three reasons. First, it helps him in his direct objective, informing himself. He is able to play what he has learned against the additional analysis of these experts, thereby stretching himself further. Second, he establishes implicit understandings regarding future times when he may call upon their services again. He tries to make clear that their time has not been wasted. He has used their advice and counsel and will give them the benefit of insights he has received that they may never personally share. In other words, he'll help them, too. Finally, he does it as a matter of common courtesy.

"These people are major figures within their chosen fields," Kennedy told me. "They are busy with their own priorities. I want them to know that I value them, that what they contribute has an impact. I want them to know the truth—that they are special. By these debriefings I hope I have made a commitment to them, that it's not a one-way street. What I am seeking is knowledge and understanding, not for one trip or one briefing, but as long as I'm in the Senate. That's an ongoing process."

Kennedy's is a particular kind of follow-up that we could all practice. After returning from a key meeting, set aside time to debrief those who helped you prepare. That includes your secretary. Share a little of the meeting and you will be better prepared for your next one, and you will get more help from those whose job it is to assist you.

ROUTINE MEETINGS AND DELEGATION

For his weekly staff meetings, Los Angeles Chamber of Commerce President Ray Remy always reviews what was decided and assigned at the previous staff meeting in order to ensure a sense as well as the reality of following up. No one person in particular is on the spot. But everyone knows that what was discussed and delegated at one meeting will be reviewed at the next; follow-up becomes nearly automatic. Routine meetings in particular can become mere recitations of continuing problems. Take the time at these meetings to assess any progress that has been made on these problems since earlier meetings.

Norman Lear may have carried note taking in connection with follow-up to a new level. When he's in production of a weekly television show, a process that requires the creation of a new script every week, he pulls his writers in nearly every day to review drafts and make improvements. These are brainstorming sessions looking for angles on the plot or characters. Ideas can come out quickly and can be lost just as quickly. Lear does not assign a particular writer to take notes. Nor does he have a secretary sit in and take shorthand, since some of the others find it distracting, and there is a delay in getting a transcript back after the meeting. Instead, Lear has installed recording equipment into the meeting table. The recorded meeting is sent on a two-minute delayed basis to a stenographer outside the room. When the meeting concludes and as members file out the door to get back to work on particular segments of the script, the secretary hands each of them a typed transcript of the meeting. While most of us could never afford Lear's approach, it's important to get back to people with a summary of actions taken and work assigned as soon as possible, before memories begin to fade. Especially when work has been delegated at the meeting, a written communication reinforces and clarifies the assignment.

Whatever your own solution, follow-up is just as important as the meeting itself. Don't leave the meeting until assignments are clear. Then schedule a time relatively soon after the meeting to review what you need to do to ensure that what was intended at the meeting is actually being completed.

CAPITALIZING ON GAINS

Every decision can be strengthened by virtue of how it is described. Therefore, every time you are required to summarize a decision or action taken at a meeting, it is an opportunity to advance your cause or interest. Even if you view that interest simply as reflecting accurately what took place, it is still an opportunity for you. The victory you have won in a meeting is not worth much if you don't make use of it. Always ask yourself how you can use the results of the meeting to further your cause when the meeting is over.

RECOUPING LOSSES

Likewise, every decision can be weakened by how it is described and by what action is taken thereafter. If a decision against your interest has been reached, seek to postpone implementation. If you cannot do that, perhaps you can become a part of the implementation, crafting it to meet certain of your goals. In any event, remember that there are no final victories and defeats. Said the military theorist Clausewitz, "Even the final decision of war is not to be regarded as absolute."

CHAPTER TWENTY

More Important Than You Think: Rules, Customs, and Protocol

MEN ARE NEVER MORE OFFENDED THAN WHEN WE DEPRECIATE THEIR CEREMONIES AND USAGES. SEEK TO OPPRESS THEM, AND IT IS SOMETIMES A PROOF OF THE ESTEEM WITH WHICH YOU REGARD THEM; DEPRECIATE THEIR CUSTOMS, IT IS ALWAYS THE MARK OF CONTEMPT.

—Baron de Montesquieu

ALL meetings have explicit and implicit rules. They can be as technical and formal as *Robert's Rules of Order*, the standard work on parliamentary procedure. They can be as sophisticated as the protocol at a state dinner. And they can be very confusing when we meet with people whose customs and cultures are unfamiliar to us. Rules, protocol, and etiquette in any meeting can be as important to winning as substance. Often you can't get in the game if you don't know the rules. Often you're severely handicapped in dealing with those who do.

In general, assume that your meeting partners are more sensitive to the rules and protocol than you are.

Assume there are practices that attach to other cultures that are as telling to its members as a limp handshake or crude language may be to you. As you move up your career ladder, expectations about your familiarity with these practices increase dramatically, and you will be judged in part on your ability to manage meetings among more and more sophisticated and varied participants.

In meeting with foreigners in their countries or in our own, you should, of course, be thoroughly informed not only about their customs, but also about the often subtle differences in the ways they do business. Customs and business conduct also vary greatly in the different regions of our own country. So again be informed and be prepared. But whenever a meeting takes place, there are a number of commonsense courtesies that should not be forgotten.

INTRODUCTIONS

An introduction brings a person into a social group or a meeting and therefore makes a statement about relative status as well as common courtesy. In making an introduction, you are performing a ritual that provides an opportunity for one person to know another person of equal or higher rank. Thus, you should introduce (provide an introduction for) the new employee *to* the president of the company. Introduce a younger person *to* an older person. Introduce a nonofficial person *to* an official person. Introduce a fellow executive *to* a customer or client. In other words, you should introduce a person *to* the person to whom you wish to demonstrate the most courtesy and deference. To help further communication, try to explain something about the persons you are introducing. For example, "Ms. Boggs, I'd like to introduce to you my new secretary, John Smith. John, this is Ms. Boggs, the vice president of our Minneapolis office."

You are responsible for introductions if (1) you are hosting or chairing a meeting; (2) you are the only one who knows the parties; or (3) the appropriate person fails to make introductions. If for whatever reason an introduction is not forthcoming, it is perfectly acceptable to introduce and identify yourself.

PICKING UP THE CHECK

A former employer told me, "The cheapest business expense you'll ever have is picking up the check at a lunch meeting. You demonstrate courtesy and authority in one gesture, and your lunch partner will feel he owes you something."

More important is knowing when you must pick up the check. A friend of mine tells the story of a business executive who was interested in a cabinet post or ambassadorship in the new Carter administration. He invited the national finance chair of the Democratic party, a number of influential political types, and two or three other key business leaders to a lunch. The participants all knew each other, and it was understood that the purpose was to strategize on the executive's possible appointment. When the meal was over and the check arrived, one of the participants graciously suggested that they all split it, thinking that the executive would not possibly agree. He did. It was a joke among the participants for years, but this social error was also taken as a serious lack of judgment. As one person said, "He would not be my choice for a diplomatic assignment."

It is implicit, in most cases, that the person who issues the invitation will also pay the check, including a woman who invites a man. That same person should also act as host during the lunch, attentive to the pleasure and comfort of his or her guest. A good waiter will pick up such signals and present the check to that person. To avoid possible confusion, you can also say, "May I [not we] have the check, please?" or tell the waiter in advance. A battle over a check or how it should be divided will impress no one.

BEING ON TIME

I have a business associate who is always late for meetings. It's a bad habit, one he seems incapable of correcting. When we have meetings with each other, his consistent tardiness is the subject of jokes and good fun. But I've also told him that he is making an impression on others that is not so funny. Your meeting partners want to be liked, respected, and appreciated. By establishing a meeting time, you've made a commitment. You've said that what you want is important enough to require your meeting partner to build his day around you. Showing up late is not a sign of affection, appreciation, or respect. It's an insult. And when you're late, you've added one more complication, almost never in your favor. In essence, you've given the theater critic a reason not to like the coming show.

Equally dangerous for you is the conclusion that your meeting partner will draw regarding the personal qualities of someone who is late to meetings. The message is that you are not capable of meeting your other commitments and managing your business. That's not a pleasant message, but it's a reasonable one. Your meeting, which may amount to only 10 percent of your day, is actually 100 percent of your partner's experience with you.

ARRIVING LATE ON PURPOSE

Of course, there are times when your strategy calls for your late arrival—to display or enhance your power, for example. You may also want to avoid premeeting conversations. But there is a difference between not arriving early and arriving late. And those occasions where you can afford to seek pure power are fewer and farther between the more competent the people with whom you're dealing. The most powerful and successful people I know are on time, and they expect others to be as well.

SEATING FOR BUSINESS ENTERTAINING

The rules for business entertaining are numerous, but because seating is perhaps the most obvious statement you can make—and because so many unintended in-

sults are given by unknowing people—here are a few
key points to remember.

At a formal dinner to which spouses are invited, the
host husband and wife sit opposite each other. The
most important male guest should be seated to the
wife's immediate right; the second most important
male guest should be seated to her left. Many a boss
has been insulted by an employee who gives him the
"worst" seat. The most important female guest should
be seated to the husband's right and the second most
important female guest to his left. At less formal parties, the seating can also be less formal, often at two or
more tables. Still, care should be taken to see that important guests are given appropriate deference, but
that everyone has an opportunity to meet and converse, and that no one feels left out.

COMMON COURTESY

"Life is not so short," said Ralph Waldo Emerson, "but
that there is always time for courtesy." That's good advice for any meeting, and not just because it's nice to
be nice. There's a practical reason as well. Being courteous allows you more freedom to be as tough, demanding, and direct as you require. Being courteous
allows your argument to be seen in the best light possible; it allows you some room to make mistakes without incurring immediate enmity from your meeting
partners; and it is a tool of persuasion in itself, for
many are persuaded more by manner than reason.

Look to do little things for your meeting partners. A

powerful chief executive I know makes it a habit to pour the coffee in negotiating sessions and with subordinates in weekly staff meetings. He is gaining points with his peers and putting his subordinates at ease.

You should work hard to understand the simple courtesies appreciated by your meeting partners. Reflect an appreciation for their modes of behavior and etiquette. Go out of your way to compliment when compliments are due. It's not only for them, it's for you. Here are common courtesies to remember in dealing with meeting partners:

1. Listen attentively.

2. Give credit when due.

3. Accept blame for the group if you are the leader.

4. Make sure the meeting environment is conducive to good work and comfort.

5. Show concern for the welfare and personal life of any person with whom you meet regularly.

6. Don't praise yourself.

7. Don't embarrass others in public.

8. Go out of your way for newcomers and loners.

9. Always introduce people in a timely fashion.

10. Learn to give and accept a compliment.

11. Be thoughtful of others' schedules when you schedule a meeting, and schedule well in advance.

12. Arrive on time and begin on time.

13. As a junior participant, don't sit until asked to do so.

14. Rise when an outsider enters the meeting.

15. Use formal names until you are encouraged to be familiar.

Robert's Rules of Order

No one who chairs a meeting should be unfamiliar with the basic concepts of *Robert's Rules of Order*. While most meetings are not conducted pursuant to these parliamentary rules (with the exception of annual stockholder and board of directors meetings), almost everyone at one time or another must confront them. In addition, some meetings seem to slip in and out of *Robert's Rules* depending on the circumstances. Nothing can destroy a meeting so much as incompetent use of *Robert's Rules*, and nothing reflects so obviously on your preparation and meeting skills. The participant who is both comfortable and familiar with these parliamentary rules will run circles around the unknowledgeable in both formal and semiformal meetings. And the meetings of many civic and charitable organizations of which you may be a part are run along strict parliamentary lines.

Buy a copy of *Robert's Rules of Order* and read it. For a general understanding of parliamentary procedure, the following are important points to remember:

1. A motion should be made or seconded *before* discussion of *any* issue starts. (This ensures that a subject merits discussion.)

2. The chair should restate the motion after it has been made and seconded so it is clear that it has been ruled in order. (This also provides a level of control for the chair.)

3. Reports of committees don't always have to be "approved" or "accepted." They can simply be "received" if no immediate action is desired. "Approving" or "accepting" means that all items within the report have received approval from the meeting group. Usually, the treasurer's report should be "received" rather than approved, since it is unaudited and sometimes incomplete.

4. It is customary for the chair of a committee to move that the report be received or approved. (This places more responsibility on committee chairs for running good committee meetings. It permits the committee chair to explain committee actions, and it gives the committee chair some credit.)

5. Only one main motion can be considered at a time. A main motion is the one that brings an action before the group. For example, "I move adoption of the report," or "I move approval of the minutes." (Considering two *main motions* at the same time is a mortal sin.)

6. A subsidiary motion is one to change or dispose of a main motion. For example, "I move the report be amended to delete paragraph three," or "I move that the minutes be amended to reflect my vote."

The subsidiary motion must be discussed and voted on before the main motion can be discussed and voted on, although it cannot be made unless the main motion is already on the table.

7. A privileged motion is one that calls for immediate action of the *whole group*. For example, "I move that we recess." It must be considered before *any other motion* and is not debatable. (Courtesy has a very high place in parliamentary procedure.)

8. A motion to reconsider a previous vote must be made by someone on the previous winning side.

9. When someone "*calls* for the previous question," it is only a *suggestion* to end the discussion and vote. If a single person objects, you keep discussion going. If someone "*moves* the previous question" and there is a second, you must vote on whether or not to end the debate. If the motion fails, the discussion continues.

10. As a general rule, don't attempt to draft substantive language longer than a single sentence in a formal meeting. Refer it to a committee or back to staff.

WE'RE ALL HUMAN

Everybody, from statesmen and diplomats to salesmen in small companies, corporate executives, and professionals—all of us make mistakes in matters of customs and courtesies and with parliamentary procedures. We are not born with this knowledge; it is learned through experience and study. If others make mistakes, correct or instruct them gently. Drawing attention to another's error is a discourtesy in itself. Even if you seek to make an opponent appear foolish, you only risk appearing foolish yourself. And if you make an error of custom, courtesy, or procedure, simply offer an honest apology and move on. The art of apology—sincere yet not supplicating—is the greatest courtesy of all.

Part Six

PERSONAL STRATEGIES FOR SUCCESSFUL MEETINGS

He gives nothing who does not give himself.

—FRENCH PROVERB

CHAPTER TWENTY-ONE
The Art of Listening

NO SIREN DID EVER SO CHARM THE EAR OF THE
LISTENER AS THE LISTENING EAR HAS CHARMED
THE SOUL OF THE SIREN.

—Henry Taylor

PRESIDENT Jimmy Carter had heard through his sources that his Securities and Exchange Commission Chairman, Harold Williams, was planning to appear before the Senate Finance Committee to testify against his tax reform plan, a matter of some potential embarrassment to the president. At Carter's direction, his domestic affairs adviser Stu Eizenstat invited Williams for lunch at the White House. As they sat down, Eizenstat began immediately with an explanation of the president's program. Williams kept looking for an opening, but Eizenstat spent every moment of the lunch lecturing Williams on the president's plan. As dessert was being served, Williams finally asked, "Stu, don't you have any interest in hearing what I think about the plan and why I plan to testify?" "Harold," replied Eizenstat, "don't you understand how important this is to the president?" An exasperated Williams made his testimony even tougher than he had originally intended.

Some people are so intent on what they want to say that they can't hear what's being said. But even when we aren't dominating the conversation ourselves, we all have a hard time really listening. "No one," said Henry Adams, "means all he says, and very few say all they mean, for words are slippery and thought is viscous." Listening is critical, and meeting masters are almost always excellent listeners.

LISTENING CAN CONTROL TALKING

Let's assume that you go into a meeting with the boss to discuss your new idea. He's busy; someone's just walked out of his office, someone else is waiting to go in. As you sit down he's still reviewing papers on his desk, and before you begin the phone rings. He picks it up and talks for a few minutes. You know that your time is short, so while he's on the phone you begin to edit what you intended to say. Finally you have his attention, and he signals you to begin. But you're one minute into your presentation when he picks up the ringing phone again. Now you've lost your place. As you struggle to find it, you realize that the second part of your presentation depends upon the first, but you're not sure you've gotten across the first, so you begin to repeat. The boss yawns. You can almost hear the clock ticking. You know your presentation is dragging. You try harder, but at what? You leave out some key points. Suddenly he asks you about another matter. You've changed your entire presentation; it's not clear whether you'll ever get back on track. Yet you're still convinced that your idea is a good one.

The boss has changed what you had to say by how he listened. Listening can control talking. The way a listener responds can alter the substance as well as the style of what is being said.

There are, of course, some meetings where you as a listener want to put the other guy on the defensive. If so, you can do this by the way in which you react or don't react to what is being said. But most of the time you want a real meeting of the minds, particularly with subordinates. They're already intimidated. Your task is to remove the inhibitions that prevent honesty and creativity, not create more of them. A good idea on the mind of a staff member is not made any less good because he has difficulty expressing it.

Listening with peers and superiors is just as critical. The responsibility for communicating is not just that of the speaker. Intended and unintended actions on the part of the listener can alter the presentation in such a way as to substantially distort what is being said. That's why good listening can be a very effective way to control the talking at any meeting, and good listening is, of course, essential in order to avoid miscommunication.

START WITH THE RIGHT ATTITUDE

The first thing to do is start with the right attitude. You're at the meeting with a purpose in mind. The meeting is valuable to you. Your attitude should be supportive of those who are attempting to assist you in achieving your purpose; otherwise, why have them at the meeting? Don't make it an obstacle course. Allow them to help you. Not only can your attitude get in the way of the speaker who is talking to you, it can also get in the way of what you *hear*. If you have the right attitude, it will be reflected in your manner and response and encourage the best presentation by others.

1. Don't get so caught up in critiquing the delivery or the appearance of the speaker that you miss the message.

2. Don't interrupt before the full message is delivered.

3. Don't yield to distractions, such as the telephone, a passerby, or an errant thought, or otherwise communicate lack of interest.

THINGS THAT INHIBIT GOOD LISTENING

We're all human beings, affected as much by emotions as by facts and figures. When we come into a meeting we don't enter with a clean slate waiting for input. The slate is already full of input from our whole life: ideas, values, habits, preferences of all kinds. Quite naturally, and often unconsciously, we tend to listen to things that support our feelings and disregard those that do not.

Ralph Nichols and Leonard Stevens, in their book on listening first published in 1957, called these feelings "emotional filters." These existing prejudices (predispositions or prejudgments) filter everything we hear. Often we are unaware of the extent to which these feelings distort what we hear. Words or images can activate these filters so that neighboring words, concepts, or meanings are colored. When the occurrence is obvious, we call it "gilding the lily" or "poisoning the well." But filtering is not always obvious.

When you want to win a point, you can utilize someone else's emotional filters to undermine opposing arguments or to advance your own argument. But whether you are trying to win an argument or lead a staff meeting, when the other person is speaking you must listen carefully for words and phrases that conjure up your own emotional filters and those of your meeting partners.

To help diminish the impact of your emotional filters, take stock of your own values and ideas and be cognizant of them, not so you can convince others, but because you want to know when your own prejudices are filtering the things you're hearing. Withhold your own evaluation of points made by those to whom you are listening—even when you feel yourself jump to a conclusion because of a particular thing that has been said. Seek out negative evidence to disprove your own thoughts when listening to someone else.

THE KEY TO GOOD LISTENING IS CONCENTRATION

From our earliest years we're told to "pay attention," to "concentrate." But that's easier said than done, particularly in poorly run meetings. If your meeting partners are wandering when you are conducting a meeting, it ought to tell you something! If they are not engaged, you're not holding an effective meeting. But your concentration as a meeting leader may be contributing to this. Meeting masters know that chairing a meeting is hard work, in part because of the full concentration required throughout the meeting. Before you look to others, look to what you're doing yourself.

One reason concentration is difficult is because we comprehend faster than we speak. The average speaking rate is 125 words per minute, but the mind comprehends at four or five times that rate. You can comprehend what someone is saying and still have time to think other thoughts. In fact, it's impossible not to have these additional thoughts. While you can attempt to avoid them, sooner or later an active mind will move ahead of the spoken words. Collective active minds will find different things to think about, another factor contributing to meeting failure.

You cannot prevent these additional thoughts, but you can channel them so that concentration is assisted rather than hindered. For example, use the "extra" time to think about matters directly related to what is being said rather than permit the random thoughts that will inevitably find their way in.

Nichols and Stevens suggested that you consider the following:

1. Think ahead of the speaker. Try to guess where he's heading and what conclusions he's attempting to draw.

2. Evaluate the evidence the speaker is presenting to support the points he's making. Sometimes this will

require deciphering a poor presentation or hunting for the facts. But, in your mind, try to "help him" make the arguments.

3. Periodically review what has been said up to that point.

4. Listen "between the lines" for things meant but not said, things intended to be said and not said, and things that might have been said in furtherance of the point.

In general, focus your "extra time" on fully understanding the message being delivered.

ARE YOU SURE YOU DISAGREE?

Many disagreements have to do not with what has been said, but rather with what someone *thinks* has been said. Presumptions enshroud the message. Poor presentations make it more confusing still. To limit miscommunication, offer to repeat back to the meeting partner with whom you think you disagree what he has said. Before you attack the point, restate it in its most positive sense. Then ask your meeting partner to restate your point of view.

Make sure that what you do disagree with is really relevant. You may think Cleveland is a great town; he may think it's a lousy town. But it's irrelevant if you both agree that a plant should be built in Cleveland.

THE DIFFERENCE BETWEEN
LISTENING AND CONCEDING

Some people are apparently so insecure about their own opinions that they are afraid to listen to another viewpoint. When they do talk, they want to fight everything said by the "other side." You may never find agreement with your meeting partner on a particular issue, but by failing to understand his position you will undermine the opportunities for agreement and understanding on related issues. Watch out for your own "combative listening." Try to diffuse this same combative listening in your meeting participants. Find what's positive in what has been said rather than only what's wrong. *Just because you're willing to listen doesn't mean you agree.* "There is a big difference between talking and conceding," says Warren Christopher, former deputy secretary of state and chief hostage negotiator. "Engaging in discussion doesn't mean you're giving in."

The confident meeting manager is secure enough to make listening a big priority. For the person who is leading a meeting, listening is far more important than talking.

CHAPTER TWENTY-TWO

Being There

WHATEVER THY HAND FINDETH TO DO, DO IT
WITH THY MIGHT.

—Ecclesiastes 9:10

"AT this stage of my life," says producer/writer/director Norman Lear, "the most important thing about any meeting for me is 'being there' in heart and soul as well as body. That's the highest level—giving it my all whatever meeting I'm in."

By the time you have arrived at any meeting, you've had every opportunity to avoid it or to change it. By the time you've arrived for the meeting, you've had every opportunity to determine what you want to accomplish in general and with each participant in particular. You have prepared as much as you could prepare or were willing to prepare. The issues are before you. Your role in relation to your meeting partners is established. Whether they are absolutely necessary or not, the participants are there; it's too late to eliminate or include anyone. The meeting is on.

Even if it does not appear to be the perfect meeting, it's still a meeting that will impact upon your time and

293

career. If anything, the less than perfectly structured meeting is more dangerous than the well-structured one. Judgments about you and your performance will still be made. It will require more of your attention to avoid failure and achieve success.

So now is the time for *being there*. No excuses. You'll only weaken your position. No complaints. Complaining will only undermine the meeting. You can't be anywhere else. This meeting is the only place you can be. You're here, and others are relying on you. Give everything you have to make the meeting work.

No one is foolish enough to believe he could play his best point in tennis without being totally immersed in the game. You've got to keep your eye on the ball. Meetings are no different. Having stopped everything else you could be doing to attend this meeting, don't waste it all by mentally being someplace else.

"One of the things that Jean Stapleton [of *All in the Family* fame] has taught me through the years," continues Lear, "is to try to be where I am. I don't know how many times I didn't really wake up until ten minutes into a meeting. Or I faded partway through it. I noticed very early in my relationship with Jean that she was always there. Other people were drifting, but she was always there. It's the most amazing thing about her. And watching her, I have said, 'That's the way I want to be when I grow up.' It's the highest level."

We all know people who appear incapable of devoting attention to where they are at a given time. I have a friend who is constantly leaving a meeting to take or make phone calls. I happen to know that many of these calls are hardly urgent, for he has stepped out of meetings to return telephone calls to me that were not identified as urgent. Besides the fact that he's using his time inefficiently, his inability to remain in the meeting is distracting to his meeting partners and disruptive of the meeting itself. One gets the feeling that he moves from meeting to meeting and phone call to phone call with little connection to what he is doing. My friend has a bad reputation around town based on his superficial attendance. He still wonders why he isn't given more leadership responsibility by his peers.

Then there is the friend or business associate who cannot carry on a conversation in a crowded room without looking over your shoulder for the next person he should talk to. You will almost never see the top guy do this. It's rude, insulting, and very ineffective. If you're in a one-on-one, be there until you move on.

If you're still looking at papers when an associate is talking to you, you're losing the meeting. If you're interrupting a phone call for another phone call, you're losing the meeting. If you're letting the meeting go on without contributing, you're losing the meeting.

The meeting master demands much of his meetings and more of himself. He is willing to reduce the number of meetings, the number of participants, and the time he spends in meetings. But once there, he gives his full commitment. The amateur mistakenly thinks it's a sign of power and influence to constantly interrupt the meeting or be interrupted. The master knows the importance of being there and saves any such tactics for when they might really matter. The master is always conscious of the effect his behavior has on others. If he loses focus, he knows he only encourages others to lose focus. If he appears to abdicate responsibility, he knows others will, too.

"When I've really gotten into trouble," says former U.S. Air Force Secretary Verne Orr, "is when I'm thinking about something else, when I'm not focused on what's before me."

"You know, if I didn't want to be there, I could have said so," John Tunney says. "So when I attend a meeting I try to give it everything I've got. Frankly, it forces me to make better choices about meetings I will attend, and it encourages me to do the preparation necessary to make my meetings worthwhile."

SOME RULES FOR "BEING THERE"

1. Don't arrive late.

2. Don't interrupt meetings for phone calls unless of the most urgent kind.

3. Don't leave the meeting room.

4. Don't slump in your chair or doodle or indicate your lack of interest unless that's the message you want to deliver.

5. Do listen attentively to the contributions of your meeting partners; check yourself midway through the meeting to be sure you're giving the meeting your full attention. To help, ask yourself what each item, each matter, each discussion, will accom-

plish and how you can help get each member of the group to contribute.

6. Do contribute when you can, and listen in a way that encourages others to contribute effectively.

7. Do focus hard to achieve the group good.

8. Do find what's positive and eliminate the negative.

9. Do seek to be the kind of participant you expect others to be.

Of course, "being there" is infectious. If you can be there, others will follow. If you drift, that's the tone you set for others. This meeting, like it or not, is your meeting. The more attention you give, the more care you show, the more you will get out of the meeting and the more the meeting will reflect positively on you and your business and professional life. And, like the meeting masters, you will begin to make evaluations regarding the skills of other participants, gathering around you better and better people. "There is something that is much more scarce, something far finer, something rarer than ability," said author and editor Elbert Hubbard. "It is the ability to recognize a particular ability."

A CHECKLIST FOR ANY MEETING

The following list suggests the multitude of considerations relevant to meetings. For a brief, informal meeting, only a handful of these items need be addressed. For a meeting with major consequences for your organization, all or most may need your careful attention.

IN CONSIDERING WHETHER TO CALL OR ATTEND A MEETING:

- Picture what you will want to have accomplished when the meeting is over.
- Force yourself to justify the meeting as the best use of your time and the time of others. Make sure you can be ready for the meeting.
- Be sure you have the mandate to do what is sought or required.
- Make sure that you really need the meeting to accomplish all of what you want to accomplish. Consider saying no. Consider one or more brief encounters as an alternative, or consider handling only some of the proposed issues.
- In any event, be willing to take full responsibility for your participation. A judgment will be made, and your time and leverage are at risk.

BEFORE THE MEETING:

- Be sure you are clear on the stated goal.
- Be sure your meeting partners are clear on the stated goal.
- Establish a specific standard by which you will measure success or failure.
- Determine what your *personal* goal is with the group as a whole and with each particular member.
- Reduce the number of people to only those necessary to accomplish the goal.
- Assess your basic relationship to your meeting partner or partners: superior, peer, or subordinate. Evaluate their likely personal interests and needs.
- Reduce the number of issues and tasks to only those necessary to accomplish the goal.
- Prepare more. Envision the meeting as you would like it to take place and as you expect it to take place, and determine what must be done in the way of further specific preparation to make your desired vision a reality.
- Establish a meeting environment and theater (including style, location, room size, and seating) consistent with your goal.
- Consult with any participants or others whose cooperation is necessary in order to meet the goal.
- Establish a clear and appropriately detailed

299

agenda, and circulate it and other written materials in advance.

- Do your homework, and go at least one step beyond the expectations of your meeting partners.
- Form a *tentative* judgment on all issues.
- Count the votes for issues critical to you.
- Be aware of the particular customs, rules, and etiquette for the meeting.

AT THE MEETING:

- Approach the meeting and your partners with a positive attitude.
- Arrive early and make contact with key players.
- Find the control positions at the table.
- Reflect a positive attitude toward the task and your meeting partners throughout the meeting.
- Make sure someone will be taking notes.
- If you're leading, start on time and begin forcefully.
- If you are leading, state the purpose and estimate the time for completion. This is your most important statement. Restate the purpose periodically.
- If you're leading, be prepared to separate the process from substance for your meeting partners. As a participant, watch for tendencies to mix process and substance.
- As leader, separate facts from beliefs, look out for emotional buildups, seek contributions from

all, clarify agreement and disagreement, make people feel important, protect the integrity of the group and the individual members.

- As a participant, contribute early, clearly, and often—but thoughtfully.
- Divide big problems into subproblems, and address them separately whenever possible.
- Separate the problems discussed from the people discussing them.
- Summarize periodically in the context of the purpose.
- Make your own points clearly and concisely. Don't get lost in philosophy.
- Don't waste bullets on issues not important to you.
- Whether you're winning or losing your point, know when to quit.
- Look for every opportunity to show courtesy and respect.
- Listen attentively and demonstrate your attention to others.
- Be there in mind as well as body—give 100 percent.
- Summarize what was accomplished in a positive way, and make people feel good about their attendance.
- Don't allow the meeting to go on when its work has been completed.

AFTER THE MEETING:

- Assess the meeting in terms of your original goal and your measurement of success. Keep moving toward the goal.
- Share the results with people who need to know, including those who have helped you prepare.
- Follow up assignments quickly.
- Capitalize on gains and recoup losses by follow-up memos and brief encounters as necessary.

ACKNOWLEDGMENTS

IN preparing this book, I had the opportunity to consult personally with a number of people as well as to review many written sources. I want to thank the following persons, who offered ideas or commented on the drafts: Dr. William L. Anixter, Dr. Ernest Bates, Travers Bell, Honorable Tom Bradley, Yvonne Brathwaite Burke, Warren Christopher, David Corvo, Bruce Corwin, Clive Davis, Jef Dolan, Mary Anne Dolan, John Emerson, Tom Evans, Gary Eyler, Rick Feldman, David Gardner, Duane Garrett, Don Gevirtz, Greg Hahn, Jerry Hayward, Susan Holmes, Pat Hubbard, Maria Hummer, Robert Huttenback, Mickey Kantor, Michael Kassan, Senator Edward Kennedy, Joe Kieffer, Maureen A. Kindel, Jonathan Kirsch, Les Klinger, Wendy Kout, Norman Lear, Molly-Ann Leikin, Charles T. Manatt, George McCambridge, Verne Orr, Victor Palmieri, Henry C. Rogers, Ron Rogers, Tim Sexton, J. Gary Shansby, Stanley Sheinbaum, Ron Silverman, Joshua Smith, Paul Sweet, Michael Tannen, Senator John Tunney, Honorable John Van de Kamp, Jack Van Valkenburgh, Ted Van Dyke, David Viar, Ciji Ware, Michele Willens, Harold Williams.

Maureen and Eric Lasher reviewed the earliest proposal and gave me the encouragement to go forward. I want to express special thanks to Fred Hills and Burton Beals at Simon & Schuster for their experienced counsel. Lucia Smith not only assisted with the manuscript but also offered her usual sound advice throughout. I reviewed a great number of written materials, but of particular value with respect to the relationships of meeting partners was David Hon's *Meetings That Matter*. The phrase "collective incompetence" was first used in a speech by Victor Palmieri.

INDEX

Index

Index

309

    appearance of, 49–50
    attendance at, 31, 84
    attire for, 173, 178–80
    audiences in, 175–76,
        177–78
    audiovisual aids for, 194–95
    availability for, 99
    avoidance of, 14, 30, 80–101,
        249
    background presentations at,
        44, 165
    "bad guys" vs. "good guys"
        in, 198–200, 202
    beginning of, 110, 147, 239,
        300
    "being there" at, 293–97, 301
    benefits vs. costs of, 30–31,
        34–35
    board, 25–26, 41–42, 98,
        120, 121, 130–131
    with boss, 32, 35, 39, 129,
        174, 286–87
    for brainstorming, 76, 120,
        127, 138, 193, 270
    brevity of, 195, 246–55
    calling of, 38–40, 96–97,
        110, 298
    cardinal rule for, 113–26
    as central to business and
        professional life, 12
    chair as "owner" of, 38–39
    checklist for, 298–302
    chemistry of, 152
    "closing" made at, 135–37
    committee, 55–56, 57
    for consultation, 123
    converted, 91
    co-ownership of, 39–42
    counterproductive, 13
    critical signs for, 96–97

    for decision-making, 65, 86,
        120–21, 124, 216
    deficiencies in, 98
    definition of, 14
    development of, 110–11
    for difficult situations, 88
    diplomatic, 84
    dissatisfaction fueled by, 36
    distractions in, 69, 216, 219,
        240, 295
    domination of, 155
    early arrival at, 238, 259, 300
    "early reviews" of, 176
    effective, 49–50, 95, 97
    emotional buildups in, 241,
        300
    "emotional filters" in, 263,
        288–89
    ending of, 111, 242
    as engagement, 105–6
    enthusiasm expressed in, 172
    environment for, 76, 97,
        139–40, 149, 152, 168–69,
        299
    external factors in, 65–66,
        177–78
    face-to-face, 21, 188–89
    final remarks in, 111
    financial impact of, 33–35
    as focuses of energy and
        pressure, 11–12, 49, 74,
        82, 195, 217
    follow-up, 131
    "free-market" atmosphere for,
        139–40
    frequency of, 20–21, 76,
        81–83
    general objectives of, 27,
        113–26, 127–29, 160, 230,
        240
    get-acquainted, 155

ABOUT THE AUTHOR

George David Kieffer is a partner in the national law firm of Manatt, Phelps, Rothenberg & Phillips, and president of the Kieffer Corporation, an investment company. He is also chairman of the board of the Center for the Study of Democratic Institutions, former member of the Board of Regents of the University of California, and former president of the Board of Governors of the California Community Colleges. He is married and lives in Los Angeles, California.